THE AUTHENTIC MORALITY

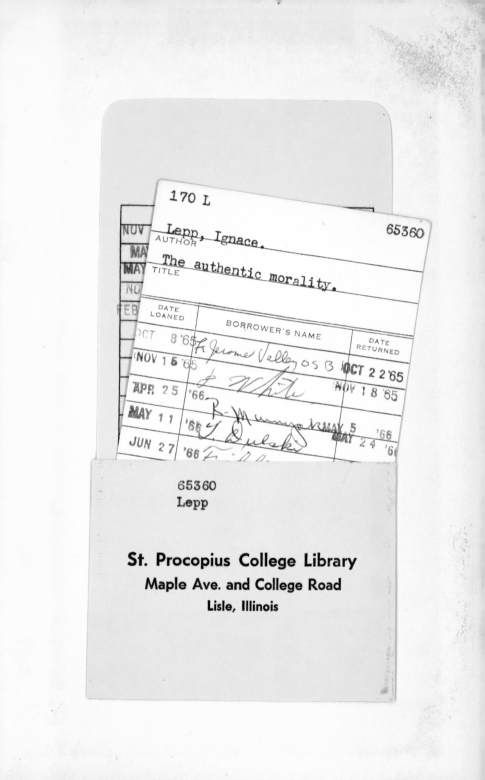

IGNACE LEPP

THE
AUTHENTIC
MORALITY

Translated by Bernard Murchland, C.S.C.

THE MACMILLAN COMPANY

New York

The quotation from "The Waste Land" is taken from
The Complete Poems and Plays of T. S. Eliot,
used with the permission of the publisher, Harcourt,
Brace & World, Inc., New York.

170

L 55mE

This book was originally published in France as
La Morale Nouvelle by Editions Bernard Grasset,
Paris.

First Printing

The Macmillan Company, New York
Collier-Macmillan Canada, Ltd., Toronto, Ontario

Library of Congress catalog card number: 65–11480

Printed in the United States of America

65360

Contents

Part I
FUNDAMENTAL PRINCIPLES

Part II
CONCRETE APPLICATIONS

The Ethics of Possibility

by BERNARD MURCHLAND

Some time ago I chatted with a well-known professor about the present moral quandary. We agreed that the proliferation of ethical theories among the academes was in a real sense a reflection of the moral confusion of daily living. We agreed, too, that the traditional role of theory was to clarify ethical problems as experienced. But somewhere along the line it ceased to fulfill this role with any adequacy. When I asked him whether or not we might anticipate any substantial progress among moralists in the near future, he shrugged his shoulders—half-despairingly, half-wisely—and said: "We'll just have to wait for a breakthrough."

That remark well characterizes our contemporary moral situation. Confusion is far more the order of the day than clarification; the quest is far out of proportion to the answers delivered; indeed, some of the questions asked hold no promise of any significant answer whatever. A large element of irresolution permeates the moral stature of modern man. The concerned layman is rightly puzzled. His moral life is dichotomized. On the one hand, he clings to bits and pieces of traditional morality; on the other, he experiments—whether timorously or boldly—with new forms in the hope that his moral being will be more firmly rooted and more happily directed. He may or may not go to church. My general impression is that he considers the churches to have abandoned their commitment to moral leadership. And in almost all respects he is right. In any event, he readily canonizes the novelist or poet who shows some way out of the dilemma (and

vii

the moral responsibility thrust upon the writer of the twentieth century is one of the most interesting aspects of our present situation). He eagerly scans the magazine reports of current mores. He ponders the message of playwrights who speak of the great destructive forces that are marshaled against us. And he reads the daily press in fear and trembling.

Implicitly or explicitly he is asking the theorist: What is the relevance of ethical theory for moral living? What can you tell us of our predicaments and aspirations? His skepticism is deepened by discussions concerning the definability of the "good," and endless analyses of ethical language. He is growing weary, too, of those existential analyses which state with prepossessing finality that the jig is up and all is hopeless, that the human project is without issuance. The new philosophies seem concerned, he says with Bertrand Russell, not with the world and our relation to it, but only with the different ways in which silly people can say silly things.

Our moral alienation is an integral part of a more general problem of alienation which I take to be one of the most serious of our time. I have no intention of going into the origins and nature of that problem here, although I think such research would be highly worthwhile. The problem is at once theological, philosophical, and social. Borrowing an image from Helmut Kuhn, we may say in a general way that to be alienated is like living in a world without signs or being suddenly transported to a strange place with no legible road signs or comprehensive language. One might recall the predicament in Bergman's film *The Silence* as an illustration. Such a world is by definition meaningless and makes man's quest for identity impossible. It is a wasteland of fragmentation and disassociation, of disconnection and despair. Modern philosophy and literature are congeries of such images. J. Hillis Miller, in his *The Disappearance of God*, puts it this way: "Modern times begin when man confronts his isolation, his separation from everything outside himself. . . . Modern thought has been increasingly dominated by the presupposition that each man is locked in the prison of his consciousness. From

Montaigne to Descartes and Locke, on down through association-ism, idealism, and romanticism to phenomenology and existential-ism today, the assumption has been that man must start with the inner experience of the isolated self. . . . In all stages of modern thought the interior states of the self are a beginning which in some sense can never be transcended."

The concept of alienation was given philosophical prominence by Hegel, and after him a number of existential thinkers. Marx made it an essential concept of our social thinking and Freud illustrated its psychological implications. A whole school of theo-logians would have us believe that the essence of our life is estrangement from others and ourselves, because we are estranged from the ground of our being, from God. But it is the literary artist who most copiously documents our awareness of alienation. Matthew Arnold saw man "Wandering between two worlds, one dead; the other powerless to be born." Kafka saw no way to re-establish a sense of presence. In our time, he said, "there is a goal, but no way; what we call the way is only wavering." Eliot, who has coined so many diagnostic images of our condition, writes:

> I have heard the key
> Turn in the door once and turn once only
> We think of the key, each in his prison
> Thinking of the key, each confirms a prison.

Perhaps Camus put it as succinctly as anyone when he says: "Man is an irremediable exile, because he is deprived of memories of a lost homeland as much as he lacks the hope of a promised land to come." The specific moral implications of this phenomenon were stated very eloquently by Kierkegaard in his *Repetition*.

My life, he says, has been brought to an impasse. I loathe existence. One sticks one's finger into the soil to tell by the smell in what land one is: I stick my finger into existence—it smells of nothing. Where am I? Who am I? How came I here? What is this thing called the world? What does this world mean? Who is it that has lured me into the world? Why was I not consulted, why not made acquainted with its manners and customs? How did I obtain an interest in the big enterprise they call reality? Why should I have an interest in it? Is it not a voluntary concern? And if I am compelled to take part in it, where is the director? I should like to make a remark to him. Is there no director? Whither shall I turn my complaint?

It is certainly legitimate to ask before such impressive evidence: Are things that bad? Have we so completely lost control of our lives? Are there no signs whatsoever? Is negativity to be our only moral touchstone? If the old moralities aren't working might it not be possible to construct a new morality? In my opinion the incontestable value of Dr. Lepp's present book is to have made an attempt in just this direction. It is also valuable in that Dr. Lepp is a Roman Catholic and a priest. A good deal of Roman Catholic morality is extraordinarily wooden and irrelevant; and people have largely lost the habit of expecting priests to have anything significant to say about moral problems. This is very puzzling when we consider Christianity's original moral dynamism and the considerable historical realizations of its initial impetus. Dr. Lepp would recapture some of Christianity's former ethical energy by rethinking its central principle of love, of *agape,* in the context of our times. With Paul Tillich he realizes that love "acts in relation to the concrete demands of the situation—its conditions, its possible consequences, the inner status of people involved, their hidden motives, their limiting complexes and their unconscious desires and anxieties." Love listens to the particular situation and opens the mind to the creative possibilities before us. Love can imbue ethics with flexibility and liberate us from the tyranny of absolutism, suffocating convention, and authoritarianism. With this attitude we can direct our efforts to a critical assessment of human nature and make morality a function of this nature rather than an extension of an essentialist metaphysics. There are no moral "essences." The Christian, perhaps more than anyone else, ought to address himself to the *facts* of human life and inquire into the extent to which these facts are relevant to moral ideals.

Dr. Lepp has the moral facts squarely in focus. His Christian convictions have been reinforced by the empiricism of modern depth psychology. And he has been especially influenced by the evolutionary perspective which Henri Bergson (and later Teilhard de Chardin) introduced into ethical thinking. This perspective turns on the concept of "open and closed," one of the most influential ethical insights of modern times. Bergson developed the distinction in his book, *The Two Sources of Morality and Religion*, which he published in 1932. Closed morality is a common, compulsive morality demanded by society for its protection. This morality is necessary as a preliminary stage in man's evolution toward freedom (and Bergson believed that the impulse toward freedom is destined to be realized). But closed morality is merely preliminary. At this level moral obligation operates impersonally and bears analogies to somnambulistic behavior.

Contrasted to this morality is that which works under the attraction of an *ideal*. Customary morality speaks for an existing order which is interested in its own perpetuation. The higher, open morality speaks for a vision which inspires in sensitive people a demand that the existing order be changed, that a higher perfection be realized. It does not normally require much effort, and certainly not much intelligence to practice closed morality. But an ideal morality keeps its vision alive at the cost of personal discipline and self-sacrifice. Thus Bergson argued that we must look for it in those exceptional persons who experienced reality deeply, to the prophets and mystics who called mankind to a truer way. Since their morality is not subject to the relativity of history and convention it is a perennial source of motivation to lesser men, a beacon on the frontiers of the moral universe guiding us to ever greater perfection.

Bergson believed that man could rise above the static, inbred patterns of a closed morality in closed societies by recovering in his own self, through the exercise of his mystic and imaginative faculties, the original vital impulse (the famous *élan vital*) and thus progressing toward higher unity and greater freedom. He was naturally distressed by the recurring forms of slavery and alienation. But he believed that a faith in the possibilities of things could, and indeed would, in the final analysis, establish a divine reality of universal love. In some typical lines, he writes:

Mankind lies groaning, half crushed beneath the weight of its own progress. Men do not sufficiently realize that their future is in their own hands. Theirs is the task of determining first of all whether they want to go on living or not. Theirs the responsibility, then, for deciding if they want merely to live, or intend to make just the extra effort required for fulfilling, even on their refractory planet, the essential function of the universe, which is a machine for the making of gods.

Dr. Lepp, with a helping hand from Teilhard de Chardin and his own experience as a psychologist, has fruitfully integrated the Bergsonian *Weltanschauung* with the Christian principle of love and redemptive hope of a universal kingdom of all men. I myself would not be prepared to adopt his theory of evolution and the noosphere as a fact. For it is by no means conclusively documented that there is such a thing as moral progress. But it is certainly a respectable hypothesis, one that accounts for a large number of facts about human nature and ethics, enables us to make desirable predictions and plot the course of our collective lives accordingly. Above all, it effectively focuses our attention on what morality basically is, namely, a dialectic of fact and possibility, of the actual and the ideal. As human beings we function in terms of ideals and life is a progressive and aesthetic translation of stated ideals into lived experience. Plato's *Symposium* is a *locus classicus* of such a view of human nature. There is at each stage of life and in each circumstance a suitable goal for human activity. Further, such goals are hierarchical, leading to what Plato called the vision of absolute beauty. Now the art of life, the ethical project, is first of all to select proper goals and ideals; secondly, and this is likely to be the more difficult, there is the matter of determining how they shall be effectively and harmoniously incarnated in lived reality.

Christianity extended the wholeness of this view. The doctrines of the Incarnation and the Eucharist, for example, were supremely suited to imprinting the sign of order upon reality and relating man to effective ideals, to a meaningful totality. But it is a matter of historical record that Christianity quite early compromised its own ideals. It did so significantly when it fell heir to the spirit of the Roman Empire and began to develop a religious and moral imperialism that still very much determines our typical modes of thinking and acting. Stoic virtues, well adapted to a policy of domination, vied for precedence with the evangelical virtues of redemption. Henceforward official Christendom was to speak much more in Christ's name than with his voice.

The moral dilemma today cries out for a reconstruction of the Christian ethic. Dr. Lepp is one of the few, and they are surprisingly few, hardy spirits engaged in this enterprise. He gives substance to our hopes for better things and indicates what we might accomplish in the way of moral renewal.

Author's Preface

I am aware that when we speak of a "new morality" we court the contempt of many and the open hostility of most of those who are by profession the custodians of morality. The Christian world, however unconditional be its adhesion to the dogmas of its faith, can on occasion lend an understanding and even sympathetic ear to those who criticize or deny its dogmas; but its members are unanimous in protest when matters of morality are touched upon. I myself have had occasion in several of my books to suggest interpretations of the Incarnation, the Eucharist, and Original Sin that were scarcely traditional. The theologians who reviewed these books obviously took note of my "errors." But, with very few exceptions, they did so with great courtesy, indeed often with a visible sympathy for my efforts to understand Christian revelation from the point of view of a man of the twentieth century.

Two years ago I published a short article in a journal pointing out that some of our commonest prescriptions for sexual morality have little justification either rationally or religiously, that there are merely vestiges of ancient taboos. What an outburst! Numerous religious gatherings accused me of wanting to undermine the Church, the family, and the state. The journal in question was bitterly criticized for publishing so destructive and anti-Christian an article. Yet I had expressed myself with extreme moderation, even in discussing those ideas which today are almost unanimously accepted by biologists and psychologists. On the other hand, I knew a number of my most vehement critics; in private they deplored the bad moral effects of sexual taboos much as I did and in language not unlike the language I had used in my article. Those among them who were confessors or spiritual directors endeavored conscientiously to deliver the faithful who came to them from the dominion of such taboos. Yet it seemed intolerable to them that the matter could be discussed in public for fear that the public confuse authentic moral values with outdated taboos and reject the former with the latter.

A little careful reflection indicates why such reactions are understandable. To be sure, theologians consider the dogmas of religion incomparably more important than the prescriptions and interdictions of morality. But they also know that most of the faithful do not grasp the existential meaning of the dogmas, however firm their attachment to the traditional formulas of the faith may otherwise be. It is a quite different case with morality. For to morality falls the task of regulating and orientating the daily, concrete life of individuals and collectivities. To cast discredit or doubt upon the value of one or another moral prescription is, so it is thought, to wish to shake the whole edifice of human civilization and deliver the world up to destructive anarchy. We are accustomed to conceiving morality in a monolithic fashion; we are afraid to question any of its elements lest the whole edifice crumble.

We can therefore understand the fears and apprehensions of the guardians of moral order. If we thought these were acquitting themselves of their responsibilities in a satisfactory manner we would hesitate to propose a "new morality" even if, intellectually, we were well fortified with arguments against the old. We have no penchant for purely speculative discussions and readily admit the primacy of existential values over abstract truths. It does not matter to us, for example, that collective property be theoretically more ideal than private property; what matters is which form best insures the concrete good of man.

But an enormous abyss separates the concrete reality of the modern world from those moral principles which everyone more or less professes. We shall see that this is the principal cause of the profound moral crisis that civilization is presently undergoing, to the point of endangering the future of the human race itself. It is not a question of criticizing the value of commonly agreed upon moral principles *in themselves*. Indeed, *in themselves,* they are excellent; to this excellence humanity owes a large part of its cultural progress. Traditional morality, and particularly Christian morality, has not become ineffective or outmoded; men today are different, partially because of the very progress traditional morality enabled them to achieve. The principal criticsm we direct against the moralists is that they have not been sufficiently attentive to the changes that have taken place in the human psyche, that consequently they have not known how to effect the indispensable adaptations and renewals in moral doctrine and in the teaching of it. The English writer Galsworthy once said: "To teach Johnny Latin it is more important to know Johnny than to know Latin." This is true for all teaching and especially true with respect to moral education.

Our purpose is obviously not to elaborate any kind of moral theory that would tend to justify thermonuclear war, torture, hypocrisy, generalized adultery, and other current practices of our times. To be sure, the science of mores ought to take these facts into consideration and seek some explanation of them. But it is a mistake fraught with serious consequences to postulate that the science of mores ought to be substituted for normative morality. It is easy enough to observe that such and such a behavior is the most generalized in a given social group; yet this does not give us the right to affirm it is either the most moral or the most normal. There is no doubt that the moral progress of humanity, insofar as this exists at all, was generally the work of those nonconformists who dared break with the general practices of their milieu. We need only remind ourselves of the moral revolution effected by the Sermon on the Mount which so scandalized Christ's contemporaries.

The novelty of the "new morality" will in no way be a reversal of moral values. I am convinced—and hope to demonstrate in this essay—that war in general and nuclear war in particular, certain forms of property, and certain sexual practices are and remain immoral and must be fought in the name of morality. But for such combats to have some serious chance of success it is not sufficient that the morality in whose name they are undertaken be sublime in its theories; it is important that it be efficacious. In order that men decide to translate into action the most beautiful and most just principles they are taught, such principles must awaken the deepest possible echo in their psyches. Now such an echo can only be produced in a language comprehensible to men of our time. It is not merely a question of vocabulary. There are numerous concepts that had deep existential meaning for our ancestors but no longer retain it for us. We are probably neither better nor worse than our ancestors; we are simply different. The tendency to generalize, natural to the human spirit, leads us to conclude that because this or that traditional principle is inadequate to the modern condition then the tradition itself ought to be rejected. But no human life is possible without a morality, with norms that guide choices by means of which must be realized a being who transcends the rigid laws of determinism.

Our first purpose is to point out what can and must be considered permanent in traditional morality and, secondly, to distinguish those superfluities which were conditioned by a given stage of human evolution. The permanent principles, supposing we succeed in establishing such, must evidently remain as intact in the new morality as in the old. The new morality will differentiate itself from the old in terms of applications and new historical and psychological incarnations.

The totality of precepts and interdictions that civilized humanity calls *morality* ought not be conceived as the immutable heritage of a given revelation; for it has been progressively constructed over the ages. Certain parts of this totality are as relevant to the man of today as to the man of the Middle Ages or the man of the Renaissance. Others appear to us completely outdated. There are some which correspond only to the Western mentality while others are equally valid for our brothers in Africa or Asia. Such distinctions in no way imply a relativity, and therefore a dissolution, of morality. Of its nature morality can only be universal; but this universality ought not be abstract. It must be concrete, that is to say it must take into account the particularities of which it is composed. We are firmly convinced of the unity of the human species. This is not, however, something already given so much as something to be realized. The same is true of the universality of morality; it can never be fully accomplished until human unity is realized.

Our *new morality* will therefore be much less novel than a timorous reader might at first have suspected from the title. However our effort is not intended to be merely an abstract one of setting forth the great principles of morality. In the second part of the book we will attempt to apply these principles to a number of concrete realities of the contemporary human condition: war and peace, assassination and torture, property and work, truth and falsehood, and so forth. We hope the reader will not be surprised to find us treating the various moral problems of sexuality in a rather succinct manner at the end of the book. The survival of ancient taboos in the subconscious of even the most libertine of civilized men causes the word "moral" to evoke for many an immediate association with sexual prohibitions. Now nothing could be more false. Sexuality is one condition among many others of the human situation. But it is the human condition in its totality that must promote morality; sexual morality must therefore be looked upon as an integral part of a total morality. Contrary to the opinion of certain psychoanalysts and other "pansexualists," it is not even the most important part of morality and its importance decreases with the development of the noosphere. However this is no reason to depreciate it or in any way avoid the very important problems that are raised by the adaptation of sexual morality to the present level of human development.

Part
∾ I ∾

FUNDAMENTAL PRINCIPLES

CHAPTER 1

The Moral Crisis of Our Times

IT CAN scarcely be denied that humanity, and I mean the evolved fraction of humanity, is presently going through one of the most profound, if not the most profound, moral crisis of all times. This poses a serious threat not only to Christianity or Western civilization but to human civilization in general, indeed to the future of the human race itself. Probably never before have men been so keenly conscious of how little it would take to snuff out human life which has existed for so many millions of years and has borne such marvelous fruits. It is true that other ages trembled before the prospect of an imminent end of the world. But they anticipated this catastrophe from an outside source, whether from some natural cataclysm or from an apocalyptic divine punishment. Today catastrophe seems to us to depend directly upon the good or bad will of men themselves. And it is precisely this that enables us to speak of a moral crisis.

In adopting this pessimistic view of the present state of morality, we are thinking of such phenomena as the extraordinary diffusion of "leather jackets" and other bands of young hooligans who manifest such a total contempt for human life, who steal and kill without any effort to justify themselves even subjectively. The communists tried to see in this a typical example of bourgeois decadence; but similar gangs are to be found in communist countries—the *houligans* in Poland, for example, and the *stilyagis* in Russia itself; the evil doings of the latter are very much a match for those of Western countries. It is infinitely sad to note that the communist revolution, which cost so many people so much suffering and sacrifice, has not succeeded in presenting history with *the new man,* exempt from the original sin of egoism and entirely orientated toward the hope of happier tomorrows.

Yet vandalism, whatever its form or whatever name it assumes, represents only a minor symptom of the moral crisis today. There are more serious manifestations. I am thinking in the first place of Hitler's death camps, the crematory ovens, and the solemnly proclaimed intentions of the chiefs of a great, cultured nation to exterminate entire peoples: Jews, Tziganes, Polish. I am also thinking of the monstrous crimes of Stalin, which were applauded not only by the majority of Russian leaders, whom we may suppose to have been terrorized by fear, but also by many men and women of the so-called free world who did not even have the excuse of fear. Nor let us forget the decision so coolly taken by the leaders of the United States of America, their professed Puritanism notwithstanding, to drop the atomic bombs on Hiroshima and Nagasaki—cities which were in no sense of the word military objectives and whose victims could be none other than peaceful civilians.

Do these horrors belong to a past that will never be repeated? May we consider them a manifestation of a passing madness? One would like to have hoped so at the end of the war. But that it would have been a delusion to so hope was soon made apparent. We have only to recall the inhuman "techniques" so widely used in recent wars of decolonization. What are we to think of those officers, certainly cultured and even refined, frequently professing a fervid Christian faith, and yet guilty of crimes so heinous that they are unmentionable? Chiefs of highly civilized states make explicit profession of their Christian status and are in no way ignorant of the apocalyptic horrors that would follow a thermonuclear war; yet they nevertheless feverishly prepare for it. And the leader of the Communist bloc, who declares himself exempt from the evils of capitalism and pretends *to make man the supreme being for man,* brandishes before crowds, delirious with enthusiasm, military weapons of presumably greater destructive power than those of the West.

Nor is this all. While the countries of Western Europe and North America produce an overabundance of food commodities and many other goods, finding it "necessary" on occasion to destroy massive amounts to maintain "the balance of market," in Asia and Africa as well as in Latin America hundreds of thousands of human beings do not have the strict minimum necessary to sustain life. And here again it is not possible to make capitalistic rapacity solely responsible for this scandal because the solidarity between rich and poor is scarcely more authentic in the communist world. While the Soviet Union wastes immense riches for the ends of war and subversive propaganda, famine is widespread in China and the starkest misery reigns in Poland, Rumania, and elsewhere.

Sociologists, psychologists, moralists, and other specialists in the sciences of man must ask themselves for an explanation of this apparently unlimited triumph of immorality, both private and public. There can be no question of blaming it upon a lack of moral principles and theories. As we already indicated most statesmen, economists and citizens of the Western world adhere more or less explicitly to Christian morality; with few exceptions, such as Nietzsche and some of his followers, they admit the exceptional grandeur of this morality. Those who do not wish to accept the Christian code have at their disposition a *lay morality*, more or less of Kantian and pragmatist inspiration, which a number of eminent thinkers have endeavored to render imperative. Moreover, Marx, Engels, and Lenin laid the groundwork for a communist morality which approved neither vandalism, nor the thermonuclear extermination of peoples, nor the famine of which Chinese children are dying. There are many works, both recent and ancient, that attempt to justify and make attractive the Christian, lay and communist moralities. They are taught in schools, churches, and cell study groups. But we are forced to recognize the practical inefficacy of these moralities, at least as far as the majority of our contemporaries are concerned. Nevertheless, under the pain of disintegrating and perishing, no human society can dispense with a morality whose imperatives are freely accepted by at least a strong majority of its members and imposed by constraint, in the name of the common good, on a recalcitrant minority. We do not propose to create a totally new morality, whether Christian or lay, to replace the ancient moralities whose practical inefficacy we have noted. I am convinced that the moral truths of the past are always true and that it would be presumptuous to invent new moral principles. It is further quite significant that between the Christian, lay, and communist moralities—and even Islamic and Confucian moralities—the points of convergence are infinitely more numerous and fundamental than the points of divergence. Whether they are spiritualist or materialist all appeal to generosity and altruism. It is true that there have been some isolated, paradoxical efforts to erect a morality upon a basis of *sacred egoism,* respect for which was reputed to promote the welfare of all egoisms. But I do not think, apart from the inventors of these systems, that many men believed in their truth or their efficacy. What the world has urgent need of is not a new moral system, but rather the means to render the existing systems efficacious. The *new morality* we will attempt to define in these pages might be adopted by adherents of lay morality, indeed of communist morality, quite as readily as by Christians to the degree that all of these moralities tend to promote man and mankind and also enlist to this end the energies of generosity with which modern man is as abundantly endowed as were his predecessors.

It is not enough to note the extent and depth of the present moral crisis and the incapacity of those moralities which are preached or taught to remedy the situation. It is highly important to establish the principal causes of the crisis. It seems to us that first among these causes is the individualism that has held such dominant sway over Western man during the past few centuries from whose consequences we are still suffering. No morality is possible within individualistic perspectives. Of course, we are not denying that each individual has moral duties peculiar to him alone and we shall point out several of these in due course. But between the recognition of the *individuality* of each human destiny and individualism there is an abyss. Since his appearance upon the face of the earth man has always been a social animal, to use Aristotle's phrase, that is to say *sociality* is a fundamental characteristic of man. Morality ought, it goes without saying, to enable us to realize all our potentialities as men; but this end can be achieved only on condition that we assume fully our condition of being social.

Under diverse but convergent influences, going back to the Renaissance and systematized by Jean Jacques Rousseau, the nineteenth century almost as a whole saw man's appurtenance to a society as the result of a *social contract,* each individual being conceived of as a perfectly autonomous reality. In this individualistic perspective each owed it to himself to seek his own interest and his own happiness. The unique limit which moralists placed upon this quest consisted in the respect for the *contract* which linked the individual to other individuals. It is indicative of the spirit of the times that even the Christian moralists adhered implicitly to this morality of the social contract, adding only to those duties based upon interest those imposed by charity. We can scarcely be too surprised that individualistic morality progressively became an egotistic morality. People were less and less concerned with the interests of others because, according to the teachings of the moralists, they represented a limiting influence upon the pursuit of individual good. Likewise, each nation and social class was constituted as a closed entity. Given this background can we be greatly astonished at the bitter moral crisis we are presently undergoing? What is truly astonishing is that this crisis has declared itself so tardily, in itself a proof of the permanence of moral structures among human beings.

The second major cause of the moral crisis seems to be the oblivion on the part of moralists and the guardians of morality to the true function morality ought to exercise in the existence of an ontologically social humanity. The profound transformation of the world and men as a result of modern geographical and scientific discoveries has threatened with disintegration or complete destruction the values of traditional civilizations. Instead of asking whether all these values were equally essential to an authentic human existence or whether among the new discoveries were not to be found values at least as authentic as those threatened, we have panicked. The morality preached in churches and taught in schools and in the family serves as a protection against the dangers presented by the modern world; it is invoked to conserve without discrimination the whole ancient order of things. We have confused morals and mores. All the ancient forms of property and family life, of social and international relations, as well as relations between the sexes are presumed to possess the same absolute value. To concede something to the spirit of modern times at any level is considered a mortal risk for the whole of what was called the *moral order*. This error of perspective much more than vested interest in the established order explains the conservative and reactionary attitude of most of the servants of God and other social leaders. But the purpose of morality is much less to conserve what already exists than to promote the human race to a superior level of existence.

In these conditions it is not surprising that traditional morality lost its appeal for those with an interest in the modern world or with those who, even though they retain some nostalgia for the good old days, realize that they must live in the twentieth century. There is nothing more demoralizing, in the proper sense of that term, than to be forced to admit that the morality we practice is inapplicable. Even though we should blame our own weakness or cowardice, the result is always discouragement, often a feeling of inferiority sometimes leading to neurosis. If, on the other hand, we realize that the morality itself is at fault, we then reject the most solid support a man rightly aware of his personal limitations can lean on. There are a good number of patients in psychotherapy whose illness is the direct consequence of their moral conflicts. Here is a typical example. A young Catholic

couple made every effort to follow the Church's teaching on conjugal life. They had seven children in six years. Financial, hous-
ing, and health problems were by this time in bold evidence.
Nothing seemed to work for them. The rhythm method did not
have the expected results. Complete abstinence, which they tried,
was followed by almost intolerable nervous tension together with
frequent disputes and temptations to adultery. The husband
finally accused Christian morality of being absurd and impossible
and rejected it together with the faith on which such a morality
claimed to be founded. But where could he find another rule of
life? One cannot after all abandon oneself to personal instincts
and caprices. His wife remained convinced that the morality was
right and that she was weak because she could not live up to its
commandments.

This relatively simple example indicates the apparently in-
soluble difficulties of many men and women. But there are equally
serious problems in the domains of social and international
morality. How can one reconcile the patriotism that is taught in
the schools and preached in the churches with the dignity and
equality of all men? Who is more moral, the conscientious ob-
jector who refuses to bear arms or the ardent patriot who preaches
a crusade? For many French Catholics it was deeply humiliating
to hear a military chaplain publicly attempt to justify morally
the promoters of the colonial war and its torturers. Yet nothing
would lead us to suspect this priest's sincerity. The question is
to know whether or not patriotism as he conceives it is moral,
whether or not the changes that have marked the human condition have not profoundly modified the attitude we ought to
have toward our country.

The widespread feeling that the old morality is no longer
adapted seriously compromises the universal character of morality
as such. Some eminent thinkers, in a sincere desire to afford some
remedy to the moral crisis, have come to identify morality with
mores. It becomes a question of establishing statistically the most
generalized practice in a given social group: thence morality is
measured in terms of conformity to that practice; immorality in

terms of dissidence. Thus sexual relations among single people would be moral in Sweden and immoral in Spain, and pederasty would be moral in certain Islamic countries. Too, war with conventional arms would be moral while thermonuclear war would be immoral uniquely because of its innovations. A modicum of reflection suffices to indicate how fallacious such a conception of morality is. At most the historian can observe that in the past, within closed societies that were ignorant of other social groups, morals were identified with mores. But the relativism of such a morality is seen only by the historian who views it from a privileged position. For members of these given groups it was a question of a universal and absolute morality, obligatory for all men. In the world of today, where the customs of India are as well known as those of Ireland, relativism, far from remedying the moral crisis, would only aggravate it. And it is certain that this crisis is not without some relationship to our knowledge of the plurality of moral practices.

It would be easy to list other causes of the present moral crisis. It does not seem to us that this is necessary to convince our readers of the urgency of a *new morality* and of the direction in which it ought to seek to define itself.

CHAPTER 2

Psychological Morality

We are not the only one or even the first to proclaim the urgent necessity of a new morality, one that alone will be capable of preserving humanity from the catastrophes threatening it. In the last quarter of a century numerous and remarkable works have been published on this subject. All the authors agree that to be moral man does not have to take leave of his human condition or lift himself above it but rather that he must simply act like a man. The differences of opinion begin when it comes to defining what man is.

Professor Paul Chauchard, whose preoccupations are very close to mine, speaks, as does Jean Rostand and many other naturalists, of the necessity of a *biological morality*. If this term be taken in a strict sense I fear that the eminent scholar and his colleagues are on the wrong track. The biosphere is regulated by laws whose determinism leave little place for moral action. If there were a biological morality it would be a determinist morality, which seems to us a contradiction in terms; for there can be no morality unless there is freedom, however rudimentary we suppose this to be. On the other hand, biological evolution is extremely slow, so much so that Teilhard de Chardin considered it practically completed. Thus a biological morality could only be a static morality. We could certainly speak of its deviations but not of true progress, of a veritable renewal of morality.

The most profound of the depth psychologists, Carl Jung has said that morality constitutes a function of the human soul as old as mankind itself. That is to say morality is not, as Freud thought, the more or less neurotic product of the superego; it is not imposed upon man from without by social constraint; rather it is part of our fundamental structures by the same title as the intelligence, the will, freedom, and so forth. But if it is true, and we believe that it is true, that morality is as old as mankind, it is certainly not older. We don't think of trained dogs or ants in the anthill or the lioness dying for her young as acting *morally*. Mankind, to use Teilhard de Chardin's terminology, begins with the appearance of the noosphere, that is to say with the life of the spirit, and only at this stage of evolution can we meaningfully speak of morality. While the millions of years of human evolution observable to historians and prehistorians reveal scarcely discernible biological modifications, the growth in the noosphere is immense. The present moral crisis cannot be considered as a result of a biological regression but it presents itself as a deviation or a relapse of spiritual energy.

Biology is not therefore, in our opinion, capable of providing the scientific basis necessary for a morality that must promote the progress of a humanity in the process of becoming adult. The more specifically human sciences, and primarily psychology and sociology, must furnish such a basis.

The following statement by Chauchard is thus, to our way of thinking, false: "A biological knowledge of the essence of human nature is sufficient to permit us to understand what is in accord with this nature and what is against it." And again: "Every biologist, even a materialistic one, who recognizes that the eye is made to see accepts that *finality of fact* intrinsic to the organism." It is not that biological structures are indifferent to the psychic and social lives of men. The advent of the noosphere in no way postulates the destruction of the biosphere, not even the destruction of the hylosphere. Both are dialectically assumed into a superior sphere of operation. Further, in the present condition of humanity there is a close interdependence between the biosphere and the noosphere. Such modern sciences of man as psychosomatic medicine and characterology are founded upon the scientific recognition of this interdependence. It is therefore legitimate and necessary that the moralist concern himself with the biological conditions of existence.

Nonetheless it is primarily from psychology and sociology that he must draw his principal insights. More particularly, modern depth psychology permits us to sort out the conscious and subconscious motives of our actions, to discern what pertains to the network of determinisms and what pertains more or less directly to the domain of freedom, that is to say of morality. This same psychology also enables us to observe with a good deal of scientific exactness the changes that have come over individual and social man in modern times. Thus it indicates to us the direction in which we must orientate our effort of constructing a new morality.

The moralist judges men's actions from the outside, from the point of view of the moral law, objectively. The moral law prohibits stealing; therefore whoever steals acts immorally. The psychologist is more attentive to the subjective motivations of actions. It is true that the moralist also takes into account certain subjective motives. He does not make the same judgment, for example, about someone who steals because he is in need as about someone who steals for gain. But the psychologist goes further. He is not content to establish subjective conscious motives; he endeavors to search out the unconscious motives as well. There may be various and subtle reasons why a thief, for example, was motivated to commit a crime.

Mrs. N, an aristocratic lady and the wife of a rich banker, came to see me about her son Paul, aged 30. Paul had everything he could possibly desire. Yet this did not prevent him from committing a number of petty thefts; his mother learned that he had recently participated in a burglary with a group of delinquents. She was terrified that the police would discover the culprits and the family reputation would be irreparably stained. From an objective point of view Paul was a thief without attenuating circumstances; indeed he would likely be judged the more harshly since he was the son of a rich family with no reason to steal. In the course of psychotherapy, to which Paul submitted at his mother's insistence, we observed that his unconscious need for compensation drove him to steal. He had been restricted by a too tender maternal tutelage well beyond adolescence. The over-solicitous mother had wanted to spare her son all the temptations and deceptions of life. She kept him as close as possible to her, pretending to be his only and total confidante. Paul accepted protection without protest and indeed seemed to enjoy it. But his friends at school and later in the office considered him sneaky; he played secret tricks on others and the like. This as well as the thefts he committed turned out to be his means of avenging his mother's affectionate tyranny; it was his way of affirming his autonomy.

A young woman of 19, also of good family, scandalized her parents and friends by engaging in a series of amorous affairs with older men. She was socially condemned as a tramp. But psychotherapy revealed that since her childhood she had suffered affective frustration in relation to her father. He was a reserved and strict man who was openly disappointed by the arrival of a daughter when he had expected a son. It was less sexual pleasure than paternal affection that the young woman unconsciously sought with older men. After each experience she was quickly disillusioned because she wanted to be loved as a girl and not as a woman.

Must we conclude from these two examples that neither theft nor promiscuity are immoral since the two people in question seemed to behave according to the laws of psychological deter-minism? Freudian psychoanalysis, because of its determinist pos-tulates, would be inclined to judge in the affirmative. In this view treatment ought simply liberate the subjects from their bad con-science and guilt feelings; morality is no more than a projection and crystallization of unconscious interdicts and taboos. Psycho-synthesis, on the other hand, at least as it has been elaborated by Dr. Assagioli of Florence and myself, refuses to admit as proven the thesis that all morality is the product of a maleficent superego. We have no doubt, as Jung said, that morality is *a function of the human soul as old as humanity itself.* The action of an unconscious superego certainly exists, and this precisely was at the origin of the moral deviations of the two young people whose cases we discussed above. Even supposing that the personal responsibility in these instances had been greatly diminished or even abolished, theft and promiscuity would not be less morally objectionable. Psychotherapy as we conceive it takes as its goal to liberate the subjects from the dominion of unconscious motives of the superego in order to render them capable of authentically moral behavior. For it is important to insist against erroneous opinions that are far too widespread that the purpose of morality is not to surround man with a network of prohibitions and interdictions; quite the contrary, it is to permit him to realize fully his *humanity*. Even if some psychoanalysis succeeded in liberating men from all sense of morality the result would be an inevitable and rapid decline to an infrahuman state which, out of respect for animals, we would not dare call, *animality*. In opposition to a certain kind of primitive Freudianism, our firm conviction is that the individual and collective disorders troubling humanity today are not owing to an excess of morality but rather to a deficiency of it, to the lack of adaptation of conventional morality to the concrete human reality of our times. Moral demands must lose their association with unconscious constraint and taboos; they must be freely willed by men who are aware of their duties and desirous of elevating themselves to the order of the noosphere. It is in this sense that psychosynthesis can be of service to morality and not in the sense of having moralizing presuppositions.

We see no conflict between psychological morality and an objective morality founded upon religious revelation or philosophical reasoning. Theologians and philosophers of morality endeavor to establish, in terms of different criteria, what is *good* and what is *evil,* morality being conceived as promoting the good and combating evil. The notions of good and evil have certainly

changed in the course of history but, as we will have occasion
to note, a recognition of these changes in no way implies the
profession of a moral relativity. These changes are in no way
fortuitous; they are part and parcel of the general evolutionary
development of human consciousness. Just because some primitive tribe approved patricide and considered cannibalism a sacred
rite while our morality condemns both is no reason to conclude
that our morality possesses no objective value. Only an outdated
conception of man, a conception denying creative evolution and
spiritual growth could embrace such a relativism.

Granted that good and evil exist objectively, we must add that
these notions must be subjectively felt and accepted by us if
morality is to be efficacious. In default of this the highest moral
theories will remain existentially inefficacious.

It is far from our intention to propose a psychological morality
that is purely subjective. With the praiseworthy intention of
reacting against moral legalism some preachers and spiritual
writers have put too much accent on *purity of intention*. It little
matters from a moral point of view whether we build cathedrals
or peel potatoes (the image is from a writer recently much appre-
ciated in Catholic circles); what counts before God is the intention with which we act. It is not difficult to see how such a thesis
implies a near total contempt for the world and for human
activity. To be sure, the *intention,* the subjective disposition is
essential if a human act is to be moral; the action of peeling
potatoes is not immoral but can become, under certain
conditions, highly moral. Nevertheless one who possesses the
necessary talent for building cathedrals would act immorally
if he deliberately renounced using his talent to do something
less significant.

Teilhard de Chardin reacted in a particularly strenuous fashion against this kind of morality of intention. His adversaries
have criticized him for substituting a new objectivism that is as
false and dangerous as the old legalistic morality. Who does evil
or who does not do the good he is capable of does not act morally
whatever be the purity and nobility of his intentions. Torque-

mada and his henchmen seem certainly to have had the intention and conviction of working for the highest moral good, the glory of God; but this in no way makes the chambers of torture and the butchers of the Inquisition less morally condemnable. That there may have been *attenuating circumstances* in the case of certain inquisitors is another matter that pertains more to the domain of judges, or the Supreme Judge, than to that of the moralist. On the other hand, a scholar may be motivated by nothing other than the passion for research without any explicit altruistic intention. If his labor results in an objectively good discovery, how can one not recognize the moral value of his activity? The truth is that to be authentically moral human behavior ought to be both objectively good and subjectively willed as such. This was Teilhard de Chardin's position even though in reaction to a sterile subjectivism he seemed sometimes to accord too much worth to moral efficacy over the moral intention.

Later on we will analyze the distinctive traits of a religious morality, particularly of Christian morality. It is important here to insist, in order to avoid all misunderstanding, that psychological morality in no way pretends to be a substitute for religious morality. Authentic religious morality must also be psychological in the sense that the believer does not do good and avoid evil simply because the one is ordained and the other prohibited by God but because in his soul and conscience he is convinced that the good is good and evil is evil. If this were not the case the moral level of such a believer would be very mediocre, however strict his obedience to the law of God.

The fundamental difference between law and morality is that the first is imposed from without, whether from society or from God, while the latter comes from within man himself. In principle there is no contradiction between the two. When the law is interiorized by the subject it results in morality without, for all of that, ceasing to be the law. All laws, however, cannot be interiorized and we ought not try to interiorize them all. Not to observe this rule can have the most disastrous consequences for the subject himself as well as for others. I remember how confused was a young Italian I met in Spain because the Spaniards ate meat on Friday while in Italy it was prohibited *sub gravi*. I had a great deal of trouble convincing him that the Friday fast was an ecclesiastical law—from which the Spaniards had been dispensed—and bore no relation to morality. Confusion in this domain is compounded by the fact that legislators, whether religious or civil, are only too inclined to make of the laws they promulgate moral obligations. It is true that a law may sometimes be the expression of a moral prescription, while others may be immoral; but for the most part laws are morally neutral. In the case of laws that are immoral we have a duty to disobey them while in the case of morally neutral laws we should adhere to them in conformity with their nature and importance, without interior commitment.

Psychological morality is furthermore not the pursuit of a solipsistic hedonism. As we shall see more clearly in the following chapter, psychological morality in no way establishes man in proud isolation for whom others would be a mere means to the fulfillment of his desires. As we become aware of ourselves we become aware of others and of our appurtenance to the universe. As our self-awareness increases so too does our awareness of our solidarity with the rest of nature. There thus exists no opposition between psychological and sociological morality since our moral obligations with respect to society must be interiorized quite as much as those which have direct reference to our own lives.

Human behavior is therefore moral not only when it is objectively conformed to the moral prescriptions generally recognized but also to man's subjective *state of soul*. This truth is of the highest important for moral education. An infant has no more morality than an animal. He acts in a given way because he has been directed to do so by his parents, because he imitates those around him, because he wishes to please his parents. It is only gradually that the notions of good and evil become personal to him and only then does he act morally or immorally. As the psychic maturity of man increases his capacity for moral action becomes greater.

Too, morality for its part greatly supports psychic maturity. This will become clearer when we discuss in more detail deviations and moral sickness.

CHAPTER 3

The Moral Conscience

Freud's theory of the origin of moral consciousness is well known. The founder of psychoanalysis took as a basic truth the hypothesis of nineteenth century sociologists according to which the primitive form of human existence was gregarious. No member of the tribe had any awareness of his individuality; instinct alone regulated his conduct. Then one day, as Freud sees it, a young man coveted his father's wife and killed him in order to possess her. By some miracle which Freud does not explain this patricide gave birth to guilt. Gradually the descendants of the original killer completely forgot the cause of their guilt feelings; but from that time on the knowledge of good and evil was deeply inscribed upon the human psyche. Further, like our remote ancestor, each of us desires his mother and hates his father out of jealousy. Virtually, therefore, we are all patricidal or incestuous even if we do not commit such acts. Freud attempted to analyze the complicated process known as Oedipean guilt which, at first diffuse, gradually became more concrete and affected our whole behavior, even those forms of behavior which bear no relationship to sexuality. According to this theory psychological awareness of ourselves would have its roots in the Oedipus complex. It is by experiencing ourselves as guilty that we become aware of our individuality.

One can admire the ingenuity of Freud's theory and recognize that the master and some of his disciples drew from it practical consequences that were very fruitful in therapy. But it is a myth without the slightest historical foundation. Freud spun it out of his imagination with the help of vague biblical references and rabbinical literature. His readers might well be reminded of certain interpretations given to the biblical narrative of original sin and the crime of Cain by rabbis and even by some Christian exegetes.

I don't believe we have to seek the origin of moral consciousness outside of man himself. No authentically scientific explanation can be given for the passage from the biosphere to the noosphere, that is to say for the apparition of man within the animal kingdom. The theist, with Teilhard de Chardin, will attribute it to the creative intention of God which is realized within the natural processes of evolution. Atheists themselves more and more generally admit, at least a posteriori, that a certain finality of evolution seems verifiable. It does not seem that we have to seek a different explanation for the appearance of self-awareness than for the appearance of man himself. Nothing as a matter of fact justifies us in thinking that man evolved first and then, in a kind of secondary movement, self-awareness. According to all evidence the latter seems to belong to the fundamental structures of the human being, however rudimentary it may have been in the beginning. If, as Freud's theory suggests, a purely gregarious consciousness existed in the beginning it would be logical to assume that man as we know him had not at that time yet evolved.

It goes without saying that self-awareness coexisted with awareness of others from the beginning. We do not entirely go along with Bergson's thesis that a social self was superadded to the individual self. The word *superadded* is too strong for it implies that man existed first as an individual and secondarily became a member of a group. As a matter of fact there is no distinction, at least temporal, between social and individual self-consciousness. The spirit of individualism that accounts for this distinction must be considered not as translating a normal and primitive state but as a deviation or a sickness in the development of the noosphere.

While self-consciousness is coextensive with the human condition it is not for that reason something static. In the evolved and cultivated man of today it is certainly infinitely more explicit and complex than in primitive man. Of course primitive man acted as an individual but more so as a part of the social group in which he lived. As evolution progressed man became more and more aware of his singularity in relation to the group and laid personal claim to the physical and psychic energies that were within him. Individualism with its hypertrophy of the self may be seen as the ultimate term of this line of evolution. It necessarily brought about the grave moral crisis that we spoke about in our first chapter. The modern personalist movement, numbering in its ranks such figures as Emmanuel Mounier, Teilhard de Chardin, Max Scheler, Peter Wust and Karl Jaspers, and to some extent the whole school of Christian existentialism, is a necessary and healthy reaction against the abuses of individualism. Personalism does not reject the richness of which individualism has made the self conscious. But it tends to promote an awareness of our fundamental solidarity with others. It rejects the false philosophy of the social contract.

Certain philosophers and psychologists often speak of psychological awareness, that is to say self-awareness, and moral awareness in a manner that gives the impression that two heterogeneous realities were indicated which by some error common language designates with the same word. The German language has the word *Bewusstsein* for psychological awareness and *Gewissen* for moral awareness. There is clearly a certain distinction between the two kinds of awareness; but they are not two heterogeneous faculties but rather closely convergent functions or perhaps two aspects of the same psychic function. Moral consciousness is a development of self-awareness. It seems inconceivable that at any given stage of his evolution man could have had self-awareness without some awareness of his obligations toward himself and toward others. It is not, however, by any means certain that these obligations were originally presented in the form of extrinsic laws and rules imposed by the group and its members which became progressively interiorized. Since in the early stages of human evolution self-awareness and the awareness of belonging to a group were scarcely differentiated, we may presume that moral obligation was interiorized from the very beginning. It is highly likely that social constraint, in the form of laws and regulations, came about much later when individual awareness had become sufficiently differentiated to enter into conflict with social awareness. That afterward, by psychological processes which are now well known, the individual interiorized such laws which were first of all imposed exteriorly by the society is incontestable. This has certainly given rise to deviations and abuses and has been an obstacle to the development of many people. On the other hand, such processes have contributed to the enrichment and enlargement of moral awareness and has thus served the growth of the noosphere.

Although moral consciousness is a fundamental human structure it can still be formed. All peoples, however primitive or evolved they be, have heard of the *voice of conscience*. The ancients believed that God Himself dictated His law to us through the intermediary of this voice. Today we attribute it to our psychic structures, to the interiorized moral law. Perhaps the two conceptions, the ancient and the modern, are equally valid; for if we suppose that God has proscribed something for man He could only do so by acting upon our psyche and therefore speaking to us through the voice of our conscience. But it would be a mistake for the believer to identify each imperative of his conscience with the will of God for the materials out of which our moral conscience is constructed are multiple and not always of equal limpidity.

A good part of the content of the moral conscience of the civilized man today is inherited from the distant past. Its transmission is not effected by any kind of teaching but rather by way of a mysterious heredity. Despite the contradiction of terms we are constrained to call it an *unconscious moral conscience* for it penetrates our unconscious structures and seems to act like an instinct, a moral instinct. Other obligations, which are also inherited, come from a less distant past. They are part of the legacy which the civilization to which we belong has accumulated in the centuries of its formation. To these are added obligations deriving from family, country, and Church. This whole inner inheritance weighs upon the child, the adolescent, and the immature adult very much like the Freudian superego. As psychological maturity increases, however, the network of moral obligations loses its character of a superego to become a personal moral conscience. In the mature adult this conscience takes the form of a free adherence to the good, recognized as such by the subject. His morality is personal. He chooses from among the obligations that devolve upon him from the collective unconscious, society, and the family. He rejects some, stresses others, modifies still others. But even the most lucid moral conscience in the most mature man is never entirely liberated from its ancestral heritage. Jean Paul Sartre's effort to establish an absolutely free moral conscience is a utopia, a carryover, in renewed form, of the old individualism of the nineteenth century. We must be content with an always relative mastery, but one that is susceptible of growth, of that part of the content of our moral conscience that is under the sway of determinism.

We also speak with good right of a collective moral conscience. Thus the national French conscience is quite scrupulous in some respects but quite lax with respect to such matters as taxes and theft of goods belonging to the state. The English conscience, on the other hand, is more scrupulous in what concerns the community than individual rights. The bourgeois conscience is very demanding on the sexual and family level but quite unconcerned with matters of social justice. The proletariat conscience puts the solidarity of the class very high on the scale of values and is little concerned with its obligations toward other social classes.

It is important to insist on the fact that interiorized moral obligation in the conscience is not necessarily in the form of prohibitions. The fundamental obligation ought not be expressed in the formula: "Do not act like animals" (or "like automatons") but rather: "Act like men." With individualism, which has contributed to the loss of the sense of community, the totally negative character of a certain kind of moral teaching is very probably a major cause of the present moral crisis. Prohibitions give the subject a fatal awareness of being constrained and limited, of not being able to develop fully. As long as the awareness of belonging to a collectivity was stronger than one's personal conscience the majority of men seem to have consented without resistance to the limitations imposed by moral constraint. With modern man, even though he is highly conscious of belonging to the community, his personal conscience is becoming more and more differentiated from the collective conscience. There is no doubt that this raises the risk of falling into individualism; and yet this strengthening of the personal conscience is in line with the normal evolution of human growth, the extension of the noosphere.

The principal end of morality is to help man achieve authentic existence, to furnish him the means of realizing as fully as possible his vocation as man, both collectively and individually. The imperative of justice is not: "Do not harm others," but: "Do good unto others." That of charity is not: "Do not hate your neighbor," but: "Love your neighbor." Imagine a society in which the moral conscience found expression only in prohibitions. There would be no killing, theft, or adultery in such a society. But neither would there be much moral progress; such a society would be caught in a paralyzing mediocrity. When Nietzsche fulminated with so much contempt against the *virtuous man* it was because he learned from his experience—whether true or false—that the current morality of his time considered virtue a simple abstention from evil, something purely negative. To the virtuous man he opposed the saint and the hero who did not refuse to confront the risks of life. If we are right in thinking that the primordial moral virtue is generosity then to be virtuous it is evidently not enough merely to avoid evil.

"The satisfied conscience," wrote Emmanuel Mounier, "gives

one the desire to belong to pure sects of heretics and the initiated." It gives birth to a disincarnated idealism. It is precisely this "mediocre self-satisfaction" of which Nietzsche accused the moral people of his time. Whatever be the state of our acquired moral perfection we should not follow the example of the Pharisee in the Gospel who proudly paraded the inventory of his virtues before God and compared them to the absence of virtue in his neighbor the Publican. The possibilities of growth and enlargement of the moral conscience are practically infinite, as unlimited as the possibilities of extending and deepening the noosphere. If it is conceivable that man can adequately satisfy the demands of such moral virtues as justice, chastity, and obedience, no limit can be conceivably set upon generosity which we have already called the primordial virtue. To feel satisfied with one's generosity simply proves that one is not really generous for here it is a question of the *open virtue* par excellence.

The moral conscience of primitive man embraces only his family, his tribe, his country, and his parish. He does not identify with anything beyond these. This is the stage of *closed* morality. Even in Plato's *Republic* and *Laws* true morality obtains only among Greeks. To kill a "stranger," steal his goods, and reduce him to slavery did not seem immoral to the greatest of Greek philosophers nor does it in the Old Testament. The Stoics seem to have been the first to have professed the unity of the human race and thus the first to extend moral obligation to all of humanity. Unfortunately Stoicism was and could only be the morality of a small elite.

The truly revolutionary enlargement of the moral conscience was incontestably the work of Christianity. In preaching a common divine filiation Christ and His Apostles laid the foundation for an awareness of humanity and a truly universal morality. When we read St. Paul's celebrated profession of faith—"There is neither Greek nor Jew, neither master nor slave, but the new creature in Christ."—we find it difficult to imagine just how scandalously revolutionary it was for even the most enlightened of Paul's contemporaries. Moreover, it took centuries before the evangelical revolution began to affect human nature. There is more than a little irony in the fact that the French Revolution believed that by its famous declaration of the rights of man it opposed Christianity while in reality it formulated the fundamental principles of Christian morality. Ignorance of the authentic source and inspiration of the "rights of man" probably explains why the French Revolution ended by exalting the spirit of nationalism, a phenomenon that represents a regression in the universalization of self-awareness and the moral conscience.

Today there is a relatively numerous elite that is aware of itself not only individually or as members of society but as members of a humanity that is one and indivisible. The moral conscience of these men and women thus extends equally to all of humanity. This means that they know themselves to be at one with and responsible for all men without exception, that they do not think they have exhausted all moral possibility when they do good and try to avoid evil with respect to the members of their family, country, race, or Church alone.

The evolution of the moral conscience takes place according to the general laws of human growth that govern the progressive passage of individuals and groups from infancy, through adolescence, to maturity. History teaches us however that now and again personalities of exceptional moral vision appear and advance morality in a revolutionary way. This is somewhat comparable to those radical transformations which paleontologists have noticed in the course of the evolution of life. We observe in nature, in physical nature as well as in spiritual or psychic nature, a progressive evolution and also revolutionary mutations. *Transformism* as well as *evolution* are observable and observed facts.

Thus, as we have said, the greatest of revolutions in the moral conscience was the work of Christ and there is no doubt that we as yet do not realize all of its implications. On a lesser but by no means negligible scale Confucius, Akh-en-Aton, Socrates, Mohammed, Francis of Assisi, Gandhi and others have effected moral revolutions within more or less restricted communities but their efforts have influenced the general growth of humanity. In our own day Bergson and Teilhard de Chardin have probably done most to advance the growth of moral awareness.

CHAPTER 4

Morality and Freedom

THE MORAL conscience and its problems are closely related to the problem of moral freedom. If the determinists like Jean Rostand were right in holding that man is no more free in regulating his conduct than in choosing the color of his eyes, there could be no distinction between moral good and evil; the word *responsibility* would signify nothing concrete. Simone de Beauvoir, in the name of Sartrian existentialism, writes with good reason: "What is proper to morality is to consider human life as a game which we can win or lose and to teach man the means of winning it." And again: "Freedom is the source whence arises all meaning and all values."

Here we have no intention of taking a position on the old metaphysical problem of free will, a problem based at least partially on misunderstandings. According to the determinists the protagonists of free will suppose that man is confronted, in certain circumstances of his life, with a choice to make without being motivated to act more in one direction than in another. He would supposedly choose *arbitrarily*. Now it is clear that this kind of free will does not exist. We are always motivated more or less imperiously to act in one way rather than another.

According to Freud and his disciples the conscious self would be under an illusion if it believed it acted freely. Man's moral behavior is rigorously determined by implacable biological laws. The illusion of being free can be accounted for in terms of the influence which determinism exercises upon the unconscious. If one were to make a single exception to universal determinism, Freud wrote, we would destroy the scientific conception of the world. His hostility toward all objective morality is consistent with his general system. Morality with its obligations, its sanctions and its rewards makes sense only for those who enjoy a minimum of autonomy. If it is proven that man has no autonomy how can we then fail to consider morality as a mutilation of instinctive life? Logical with himself, Freud wrote in *Civilization and Its Discontents:* "It is simply the pleasure principle that determines the end of life and governs from the beginning the operations of the psychic apparatus." He denounces the scandal of current morality for which "often evil in no way consists of what is harmful or dangerous to the self, but on the contrary in what appears to it desirable and procures for it pleasure."

I find it difficult to see how the partisans of determinism, many of whom endeavor nonetheless to give a scientific basis to morality, can validly object to Freud's theories. If it is established that our behavior is rigorously determined then we have no right to speak of moral or immoral behavior any more than we could so speak of the animals. The simplest thing would evidently be to liquidate the illusion that the self is free by means of psychoanalysis or some other procedure in order than the instincts could function without interference, following their proper mechanical laws. Social constraints could scarcely be understood in this perspective unless we see in them a kind of corrective applied to instinctual deviations.

In fact man is not man until he becomes aware and to the extent that he knows he is aware of being free. We are not speaking, of course, of absolute freedom. As Descartes said: "Man's freedom is infinite but his powers are limited." There is much truth in that, especially from the philosophical point of view. The psychologist, who is not concerned with the essence of man but with his existential situation, cannot consider freedom as a gift of nature. What is peculiar to human nature is man's capacity to become free. In moral matters especially the psychologist speaks more of liberation than liberty. The infant is clearly no more free than an animal. But while an animal can be trained only in terms of the automatic responses of its psyche a child's education must be orientated toward liberation. Even before the "age of reason" a child is aware in certain circumstances of acting freely while in other circumstances he is conscious of being constrained. The adolescent frequently experiences a kind of vertigo, whether because of joy or fear, in realizing that he is free and responsible for his actions. The adolescent more than anyone else experiences freedom as a threat to the security of his childhood. He is nonetheless very jealous of his liberty and aspires to throw off anything that interferes with his desire for total freedom. As for the mature adult, he knows that he is both free and determined, that motives and determinations are part of his liberty.

The power to become free is not found in all men to the same degree. Many reach only a very low level of freedom; consequently their moral lives can only be mediocre; they are not capable of doing much evil and certainly never do much good. Others are capable of reaching such an elevated level of freedom that they seem to be completely liberated from all determinism. But this is only an illusion. Neither the saints nor the great geniuses of humanity enjoy that absolute liberty Sartre says is the very condition of being a man. Human freedom is an island in an immense ocean of determinism. It can certainly expand but it will never absorb the entire ocean.

Concrete freedom is freedom in a given *situation*. The situation is constituted first of all by the physical reality of the cosmos which we cannot manipulate at will. Then, however free we believe we are, we must take into account the cultural, economic, and social conditions of our age. Finally, our freedom is conditioned by individual factors—the family, heredity, health, education, social position, profession, and so forth. It would however be erroneous to think that our freedom is diminished because it is situational. This is rather the indispensable framework of its exercise. Even if we could by some miracle attain a freedom that was not situational we could be quite certain that it would remain sterile because it would lack the materials necessary to its deployment. To be sure not all of the components of our existential situation are of a nature to favor freedom; some of them are the direct reason why our effort to achieve liberation aborts short of its goal. On the other hand these obstacles can stimulate a greater effort on our part so that we reach a high level of freedom. We could perhaps not have succeeded so well had our path been easier. It is naïve to believe that the abolition of cultural and economic alienations would necessarily mean more freedom for men. There would still remain the network of physical determinations as well as factors of an individual nature, not all of which are by any means the result of sociological conditions. One can easily observe that moral problems are just as acute in communist countries, whose directors avow that such alienations have been abolished, as in the so-called capitalist countries. The anarchist ideal of an absolutely free society will always be utopian.

While education favors the liberation of man there is no precise parallel between intellectual evolution and the degree of freedom. Highly civilized men can be the slaves of their passions, their vices, and their prejudices and for that reason be less free than more primitive persons. The same is true of material wealth. It fosters freedom in some, impedes it in others. Sometimes a near total lack of riches goes hand in hand with the highest degree of freedom. As a general rule, however, ignorance and want render the human effort toward liberation, that is to say toward the realization of the highest possible degree of humanity, difficult if not impossible. That is why they must be fought against in the name of morality.

Freedom is not a strictly individual good. The case of saints and genius apart, the individual becomes free conjointly with others. It is therefore not enough that we work for our own liberation; the struggle for collective, social liberation is a strict moral duty. What would I do with my individual liberty, even if it were perfect, in a world of slaves? It is true there are those who experience their freedom most keenly when they can subjugate others. But the neurotic nature of this *will to power* is only too evident. My freedom addresses itself to other freedoms and free men fight for greater freedom together.

The notion of freedom is inseparable from that of responsibility. Only someone who is at least partially responsible for his desires and actions can be considered responsible and the degree of his responsibility is in strict proportion to the degree of his freedom. It is evidently very difficult, if not impossible, to establish the exact degree of freedom and responsibility in the behavior of a given individual. That is why the work of judges who must determine the accused's degree of culpability is very delicate. How are the unconscious motives of the criminal's actions to be distinguished? Journalists frequently amuse themselves by making fun of expert psychiatric witnesses who pretend to explain, if not partially excuse, guilt with the help of technical jargon. Of course many psychiatrists do act like pedants and speak as though they possessed very precise knowledge of the conscious and unconscious labyrinths of the psyche. But in reality even an extended psychoanalysis gives us but a partial knowledge of the secrets of the human soul; this being the case not much can be said for the quick examinations and superficial testing the experts submit criminals to. On the other hand the psychiatrists are right to this extent: no man is entirely responsible for all of his actions; attenuating circumstances are attendant upon each one.

The real difficulties of establishing the degree of freedom and the corresponding degree of responsibility do not render moral judgment impossible. It only has to be done more subtly than is usually the case. We all know that in certain simple-minded people freedom and responsibility are practically nonexistent; we call them *innocent*. In more mature people it is evidently impossible to establish *scientifically* to what extent they are free and responsible insofar as these are susceptible to important variations depending on circumstances. But even supposing a man of great psychic development acted under the compulsion of a "blind" passion or under the pressure of entirely unconscious motives, and that because of this he refuses to accept responsibility for his actions, neither the moralist nor the judge are obliged to adopt his point of view. The psychically mature man, even though he is not always entirely free and responsible at the moment of acting, is generally capable of foreseeing how he will act in given situations. How, for example, could we absolve from responsibility an adult woman who shared the bed of a friend because he promised that "nothing would happen"? In the actual act of adultery her freedom and responsibility may have been greatly diminished but in creating the situation deliberately she could presumably predict the consequences to a large extent. In such a case the initial freedom is so clearly established that her moral responsibility raises no serious question. Other cases are, of course, more complex and it is a good general rule to be extremely circumspect in judging the moral actions of others as well as of our own actions. Such reserve in no way renders our moral judgments illegitimate.

It is clearly more difficult to establish collective responsibility. For centuries Catholics considered the Jewish people as a whole guilty of Christ's crucifixion under the pretext that the rabble, who had been egged on by the religious leaders, had demanded His death before Pontius Pilate. We are in general agreement today with those Jewish spokesmen who protest against the collective responsibility that has been laid upon them. The Church herself has recently removed from the liturgy of Holy Week those texts that refer to the "deicide" of the Jews. There was probably no intention here of making any theoretical judgment about collective responsibility; rather it makes more sense to see in it a response to arguments that such texts helped maintain and aggravate anti-Semitism.

After World War II there was some question as to what extent the German people as such could be held responsible for the crimes committed by the Nazi regime. The general tendency, at least in those countries that had suffered German occupation, tended to affirm a collective responsibility. If each individual

German was not guilty of genocide the people as a whole was. The suppression of the German state, the division of the country, and the annexation of some of its provinces by former victims, the dismantling of industry and the like seemed therefore perfectly logical punishments.

I do not mean to deny or even cast doubt upon the principle of collective responsibility either in good or evil. Humanity is one and the growth of the noosphere incontestably supports that unity. Much less than our distant and symbolic ancestor, Cain, are we able to refuse responsibility for what our brothers are, what they become, and what they do. Within the great human community, still in the process of development, there exist communities of less scope such as the family and the country whose unity has long been a fact. We may take it as certain that there exists not only a mutual responsibility between the members of one family or one nation but a collective responsibility of this or that family and nation for other families and other nations, for the universal moral conscience.

Collective responsibility is never total any more than is individual responsibility. And in any case it is far more difficult to determine in any precise way. In the case of the German example it is not easy to decide, when we consider the years following World War I, whether or not this people was perfectly free to establish a government like the Nazi regime. And once this party came to power were the important minority who supported it entirely free? We are not thinking here so much of exterior constraints as of those unconscious collective forces that determine the behavior of peoples far more blindly than that of individuals. Our argument is not that the freedom of the German people was nonexistent and therefore absolve it of all responsibility; more modestly we are affirming that it is most difficult to measure the degree of collective freedom and responsibility and such a task ought to be undertaken only with the utmost prudence.

Shortly after Hiroshima, Emmanuel Mounier said that the discovery of atomic energy and the means of using it for destructive purposes conferred upon mankind the terrible liberty of committing collective suicide. Henceforward, if humanity continues to exist, it will not be because it could not do otherwise but because it freely chooses to do so. The philosopher of personalism was right in principle and, for our part, we share entirely his conviction of a humanity that is one and indivisible. Even if some head of state should in a moment of panic give the order to drop a sufficient number of bombs to annihilate all life on earth, can we say that he really chose collective suicide in the name of all, in the name of humanity as a whole? I admit I know of no satisfactory answer to this question.

Ideal liberty does not consist in freedom from *all* determination and *all* constraint but rather in freedom in view of something, normally in view of something transcendent to our present state. It is only in the adolescent and the neurotic adult that we find the need for that *freedom for nothing* which Sartre has analyzed so masterfully in one of his novels. I am inclined to think that such a freedom would not be authentic freedom.

Anyone who is capable of freedom ought to ask himself: "Freedom to do what?" Since the Second World War many nations of Africa and Asia have fought for freedom from colonial domination with a heroism that frequently won the sympathy of the whole civilized world. It unfortunately seems that most of these nations and their leaders did not ask themselves what they were going to do with the freedom that they acquired at such a price. The situation in these new countries is not necessarily as bad as in the Congo but in scarcely any of them can it be said that national freedom brought with it any great social improvement. The same is true of individuals. There are great numbers of adolescents who are anxious to throw off parental protection without asking themselves what use they propose to make of their freedom. Freudian psychoanalysis for its part strives to liberate patients from their complexes and the tyranny of the superego without further considering it a duty to teach them how to use their psychic freedom in a constructive way.

Neither sociological freedom nor psychic freedom ought to be identified with anarchy, in the usual sense of that word. Freedom is a moral value, indeed one of the basic conditions of moral life, only to the degree that it promotes a superior form of personal and community life. The protagonists of a certain kind of Sartrian existentialism, and sometimes the master himself, believe they should refuse all forms of commitment under the pretext that the freedom they have so dearly won over the forces of social and psychic determinism would immediately be lost. This is merely a sophism. Only total commitment to a superior human ideal will bring about the full development, indeed the exaltation of freedom. When no such commitment exists freedom is merely an abstraction; it becomes concrete through commitment.

Many are afraid to assume the freedom and moral responsibility of their actions. In my psychotherapeutic practice I have frequently observed that many patients declare themselves intellectual partisans of determinism only because they unconsciously feel that they are too weak, deliberately, to live the adventure of their freedom. When therapy succeeds in giving them some self-confidence and they experience for the first time the joy of acting like free and responsible men they generally abandon their determinist principles.

In a collective sense the more or less neurotic fear of freedom serves the purposes of those who have dictatorial aspirations. The German people, for example, had to suffer the terrible experiences of the Nazi dictatorship to become convinced of the moral as well as the pragmatic advantages of freedom. In Spanish countries tyranny and anarchy alternate in a fairly predictable rhythm without ever issuing into freedom. The French have not had the opportunity, since the time of Napoleon, to abdicate their collective freedom. It is true they suffered the Nazi occupation but since it was imposed from without by a temporary victor it served to increase the love of liberty. However, from time to time the French people find their freedom a heavy weight and seek to discharge it upon some *providential man* such as General De Gaulle. There have been several examples of this kind of thing in their recent history. But, so far at least, the love of liberty has always won out. In any case it seems clear that for nations as well as for individuals freedom is probably never definitively acquired but must be affirmed unceasingly and conquered anew.

CHAPTER 5

Moral Progress

THERE IS a preliminary distinction that must be made between moral progress and the progress of morality. The first of these is as a matter of fact contested by many. Pessimists have no difficulty adducing much evidence from the present as well as the past to prove that, far from progressing, the morality of mankind in general is deteriorating. Further, we are all familiar with the "old timers" of each generation who complain about the immorality of the young and speak nostalgically of the good old days of their youth when, to hear them talk, all the virtues flourished. We will see shortly what must be thought about such an idealization of the past and such a denial of moral progress. For the moment let us consider the progress of morality and the moral consciousness.

The old codes of morality, including the biblical morality that is said to have been revealed to Moses, not only did not distinguish between morality and religion; they did not, further, distinguish between morality and hygiene, morality and social customs, morality and medicine, and so forth. To eat pork, steal another's cattle or wife, have relations with a woman in the period of menstruation, adore other gods than those of Abraham and Isaac—all of these were denounced as sins of equal gravity. The moral law, at this period of history, remained almost totally exterior to the subject. This indistinct and extrinsic morality still exists for children and primitive people. Confessors are aware of it. Such people accuse themselves indiscriminately of having disobeyed their parents, missed Mass, lied, of having gone to bed with dirty feet, and the like.

Little by little, principally under the influence of such masters as Buddha, the prophets of Israel, Socrates, and the Stoics, but especially under the influence of Christ and his saints, morality became interiorized and differentiated. A normally civilized person today will pay for having illicitly parked his car but he does not imagine for a moment that he committed a moral fault for having failed to observe this police regulation. In the name of hygiene parents make their children wash their hands before eating; but they scarcely demand this in the name of morality. A Catholic who abstains from meat on Friday, fasts during Lent, and imposes other penances on himself knows well it is not morality that obliges him to do these things and that someone who does not submit to such rituals is not morally inferior to him. The medical doctor may well advise a husband and wife against having sexual relations at certain times. But he knows that his advice is not moral advice.

To limit our discussion to the Judeo-Christian tradition we can say that according to all evidence the domain of morality has become much more sharply defined since the promulgation of the Mosaic law some six thousand years ago. Yet the morality we profess today includes many forms of behavior that seemed to have little to do with morality in the days of Moses or Socrates. Our present morality condemns categorically slavery and approves only monogamous marriage. Formerly in officially Catholic countries, indeed in those under the direct authority of the Pope, prostitution was morally tolerated as a social institution while today we would condemn it in the name of the dignity of the human person. Today we are very tolerant of lovers whose relationship has no social sanction; but we are much more demanding in matters of social justice.

The evolution of morality toward interiorization is incontestably the work of Christianity although the prophets of Israel and certain philosophical schools of Greco-Roman antiquity made notable advances in this respect. However, psychoanalysts like Hesnard who draw attention to the disadvantages of a too interiorized morality are not altogether wrong. The Middle Ages avowed unlimited admiration for celebrated ascetics who withdrew from the world to live in the deserts or on the mountain tops. These ascetics followed an ideal of perfection that is not unlike that of the Yogis. It was a totally interior perfection, a perfection of man alone even when he was in the company of other men. Certain religious orders today consider this the best, if not the only, form of perfection.

It is not our intention, nor is this the place, to criticize this form of asceticism or religious perfection. What is unfortunate is that it has been taken for a moral ideal. Catholics have been known to reproach the Albigensians for tolerating the most scandalous immorality among the simple faithful under the pretext that a high perfection could only be practiced by a small number of elect. With more or less important shades of difference the same accusation could be levelled against the Catholic practice itself, and all moralities that exaggerate interiorization. It seems evident that the great majority of those Christians who admired St. Simon Stylites and other heroic penitents felt that they had neither the talent nor the ability to imitate him. It is disconcerting that the most demanding moral ideal during the Middle Ages and well beyond them went hand in hand with rapine and cruelty, with a practical behavior that is condemned not only by modern-day morality but was condemned as well by the morality of that era.

The criterion of moral progress must be sought not in solitary or individual perfection but above all in relationships with others. Let us insist that it is quite outside our intention to condemn or recommend this or that form of ascesis. We have no a priori objection to the forms of asceticism various religions propose to aspirants to religious perfection. The point is that religious perfection is not necessarily moral perfection; indeed it may not foster the latter at all and in some cases may be diametrically opposed to it. Moral perfection is not measured by endurance, prowess, or heroism but by generosity. And there is no authentic generosity except in social human relationships.

The contemporary reactions against the excesses of interiorization in matters of morality seem healthy in principle. It is not enough to have a right intention, a heart free of all egoism and greed. Our behavior ought to tend toward perfection in generosity and altruism. We are evidently not trying to establish a pure objectivity of moral obligation. The intention of the acting subject is in no way indifferent to the moral quality of his actions. He who does good without intending to is morally superior, from an objective point of view, to one whose high principles never get translated into action. Teilhard de Chardin was therefore perfectly right to praise the behavior of those of his unbelieving colleagues whose work contributed objectively to the moral and spiritual progress of mankind even though their only motive was intellectual research: But it was also Teilhard de Chardin who said, in *The Divine Milieu,* that human activity "is of worth only in terms of the intention with which it is accomplished." It is not therefore a question of a morality of intention or a morality of action; authentic morality must be both at once, inseparably subjective and objective.

Those who deny moral progress make much of the crimes of Hitler and Stalin, of juvenile delinquency, and the other components of the moral crisis of which we have already spoken. Others argue that modern immorality is but a pale copy of that of the past, that adultery and concubinage were to say the least as widespread in the courts of the Christian kings as they are in the most libertine circles today, that the holy Inquisition was not less cruel or arbitrary than Stalin's purges or Hitler's crematory ovens, that the indignities committed by the crusaders were just as inhuman as those committed in colonial warfare.

The antagonists and detractors of the present as well as those of the past are both right. Must we then conclude that there is no such thing as moral progress or decadence, that men are evil *by nature,* that no serious hope of moral improvement ought to be entertained? We do not think that such pessimism is justified.

To our knowledge the Christian conscience of the Middle Ages did not protest against the behavior of the crusaders who scarcely distinguished between their undoubtedly sincere and ardent desire to deliver the Sepulchre of the Lord from Muslim domination and their individual ambitions of conquest and rapine whence finally resulted serious crimes not only against the infidels but also against the Oriental Christian communities. Nor did the same medieval Christian conscience take exception to the butchers of the Inquisition. Some of the saints we admire most for their generosity and charity seem to have accommodated themselves with little difficulty to the crusades as well as to the Inquisition; some of them indeed took an active part in one or the other. But today it is precisely the most fervent adherents of that same Christian faith who raised their voices against the crimes of Hitler and Stalin and who, in France especially, were most energetically opposed, frequently at the price of their liberty or their lives, to the bloody repressions and tortures which their compatriots employed in the wars of decolonization in Indo-China and Algeria even though the said wars were presented as crusades against communism or against the triumphant Islamic onslaught on the cross of Christ. During the Renaissance only a Savonarola and a few like him were scandalized by the corrupt morals of the Vatican and the high clergy while the elite of the age accommodated themselves to such morality without much apparent difficulty, much as the Bossuets and the Fénelons seem to have tolerated the very unevangelical morals that prevailed in Versailles at the court of the Sun King. The Christians of today are far more demanding with respect to the conduct of the Pope, the bishops, and other professional servants of God, as well as with respect to the conduct of so-called Christian politicians.

If the crimes of Hitler and Stalin seem so monstrous to us it is not that they are in themselves, in their materiality, more terrible than, say, the famous capture of Constantinople by the crusaders or the destruction of the Palatinate by Louis XIV's order, or the religious wars, or the consequences of the revocation of the Edict of Nantes. In the perspective of a rigorously objective observer the wars and other crimes of the past were no worse than those of our century; in fact those of the past were additionally aggravated in that they were often conducted in the name of the religion of universal love. If we accuse Hitler of genocide and not Louis XIV it is simply because in three centuries gigantic progress of moral consciousness has taken place.

Moreover, it is because our moral conscience is much more demanding than that of our ancestors that we cannot judge their behavior according to the same criteria we use to judge our contemporaries. The holy patriarch Abraham prostituted his wife; Moses, of whom it is said that "he was the meekest of all men"— massacred mercilessly those guilty of idolatry; Plato, the greatest of the philosophers, found slavery and pederasty quite normal; the crusaders placed chastity belts upon their wives. The somber fanaticism of the inquisitors as well as that of the reformer Calvin, in short all that shocks and scandalizes us in the past, must be judged in terms of the evolution of the moral conscience at the time. It is thus without any hypocrisy whatsoever that the Catholic today can approve of religious tolerance without, for all that, condemning in the name of morality the many venerated saints of the Church whose names figured among the inquisitors.

The growth of tolerance seems to be one of the principal characteristics of moral progress. Its development is proportionate to psychic growth. The adolescent is almost always absolute in his judgments and cannot admit that someone who holds a different opinion can also be right. As he matures man becomes more and more circumspect in his judgments, whether they be judgments about truth and falsity or about good and evil.

Tolerance has nothing to do with tepidity. The intolerance of the adolescent or the immature adult is in no sense of the word a testimony to the ardor and firmness of their convictions. Quite the contrary, it is usually because they are very unsure of themselves and of what they believe to be true and false that they cannot abide contradiction, convictions and behaviors different from their own. Some dozen years ago I met a saintly missionary, a disciple of Charles de Foucauld, who had spent a quarter of a century among the Berbers. Far from trying to convert them to Christianity his sole missionary effort was to make them better Muslims. Such an attitude would find little sympathy among Christians today and would have been totally unthinkable in the not too recent past. Yet I am in a position to attest that this priest's Catholic faith is not less ardent than that of those missionaries of former times who, for example, approved the forced "conversion" of the Jews and Muslims in Spain.

Moral progress tends toward interiorization, toward personalism. We have already noted that the morally mature man behaves less in terms of what is expected of him from the social group to which he belongs, but because a given course of action has been prescribed by his conscience. At the same time he recognizes and admits that his moral conscience is not the result of a spontaneous generation; it has its source in the collective conscience. This awareness permits him to avoid the shoals of individualism. We cannot become authentically personal in isolating ourselves from others or in reducing others to a simple means to be used in the service of our self-affirmation. The personality can develop only in the society of persons.

To recognize and respect the *eminent dignity of the human person* in ourselves and in others seems presently to be the fundamental principle of morality. This of course is no novelty or invention. Ancient philosophers and moralists have already defined it and the sacred writings of Christianity affirm it explicitly. In becoming man God manifested His love for all men; He divinized them all in some manner. However beautiful be Pascal's celebrated line which still inspires preachers today it is not quite in conformity with the traditional Christian perspective to say that Christ shed a drop of blood for each of us; it is rather that He shed all of His blood for all of mankind. In any case, for us as for Pascal, the eminent dignity of the human person is founded on the Gospel of Christ.

We may well be astonished that it has taken so many centuries for the meaning of this dignity truly to penetrate and mold the moral conscience. This proves the extreme slowness of spiritual maturation, of the growth of the noosphere. It is altogether admirable that the dignity of the human person is today recognized and professed even by those who reject the Gospel or by those who have never known it. Even materialists, for whom man is theoretically only a link within the evolution of the animal kingdom, believe him to be worthy of unlimited dedication, of infinite respect. This is not the least of the miracles performed by Christ.

Of course we have not reached the final maturity of the moral personality. If, more or less implicitly, more or less consciously, the principle of the dignity of the human person is recognized by almost all men, the practice is far from conforming perfectly to the principle. Moreover, it is precisely the scandalous wedge between the content of the moral conscience of modern man and its moral behavior which led us to diagnose the serious moral crisis that might well become a mortal illness if it is not remedied in time. In noting that an immense moral progress has been accomplished by man and that modern man is particularly conscious of the dignity of the human person, we do not wish to fall into a naïve optimism that would have us believe the essential is already attained, that the future toward which we march is necessarily made up of *happy tomorrows*. More modestly, it is our opinion that the present degree of development of the moral conscience furnishes mankind the necessary tool to construct his future. Depending on the use he makes of this tool he will bring about a better future or, on the other hand, an unhappy future. We are far from having reached the noosphere; at most we are in a position to think that we have arrived at one of the decisive turning points of its development. The moral crisis we are going through may well appear to succeeding generations as a crisis of decisive growth. This will depend largely on ourselves; for the fundamental, qualitative difference between the noosphere, on the one hand, and the hylosphere and biosphere, on the other, is that the maturation of the latter takes place mechanically while that of the noosphere is accomplished by means of moral action, that is to say by means of free human commitments.

Some doubt and even deny explicitly moral progress because it does not take place in a rectilinear manner. Like all steep inclines it zig-zags. Mountain climbers know well that in their climb toward the summit they are sometimes obliged to descend a few degrees. We learn from the biographies of men and women who have reached a high degree of moral perfection that their progress was not continuous; they too zig-zagged. The same is even more true of ordinary men and of mankind at large. Moral progress appears incontrovertible only when we take into consideration its principal stages of development.

CHAPTER 6

Natural Morality and
the Nature of Man

For a long time now, probably since the theologians more or less happily baptized the philosophy of Aristotle, Christian moralists have held that the morality taught in the name of revelation is in all essential respects a *natural morality*. They insist at great length upon this qualification for it is important for them to establish that Christian morality requires nothing foreign to man's nature. Christ, they say, certainly elevated man to the supernatural order but He began by restoring human nature to its original dignity whence it had defected because of sin. Further, if Christian morality is natural morality, Christian states have the right and the duty to demand respect for and observance of it by non-Christians. The majority of free thinkers, until very recently, made theirs this idea of natural morality. It was a point of honor with them to prove by their conduct that man needed no revelation or mysticism to observe natural morality integrally. The funeral eulogies of many Free Masons stressed their character of "lay saints." It has only been recently that lay morality has made a selection from among the traditional principles and precepts—rejecting those which seemed to be of specific Christian origin and retaining those which were considered intrinsic to natural morality.

Christian morality is far from being the only one to claim the status of natural morality. The disciples of Mohammed and Confucius, indeed of Marx and Lenin, claimed the same status. For a long time the controversy between moralists of different schools had as its object to *prove* that such and such a precept of the adversary's position was not *natural* while the teaching embodied in their own position was completely so. One party tended to stretch the domain of natural morality to the limit while the other party restricted it to a minimum.

It is clearly impossible to make any definite pronouncement about natural morality until we have first defined the nature of man. For centuries philosophers, theologians, and moralists considered it, as it is sometimes considered today, as something essential, immutable. In this perspective it was at least theoretically possible to make an exact inventory of human nature and establish scientifically what was natural and what was not. Quite naturally, following a spontaneous inclination of the spirit, each thinker took as a model of human nature what he observed in himself and in those about him who belonged to the same race and the same civilization as himself. Thus the Greeks thought non-Greeks were *barbarians*. The Jews considered those who did not profess the Mosaic law as *Gentiles*. And Christians have only recently stopped referring to Muslims, Hindus, and members of other highly structured religions as *pagans*.

In these circumstances it is not surprising that many superior spirits whose horizons transcend narrow national, racial, or confessional boundaries are more and more tempted to deny the very existence of a human nature and, by way of consequence, the existence of a natural law and morality. Simone de Beauvoir is the spokesman of many when she writes: *"It is impossible to propose a morality to man if we define him as a nature, as something given."* If it were truly impossible to define human nature we would side with Simone de Beauvoir and attempt to elaborate a morality that would be, if not the negation of nature, at least transcendent to it.

But it would be very risky to propose a morality that abstracted from the notion of a human nature, that lost all normative power, all universal character, that would only be a simple part of the science of mores. But it is not merely these pragmatic considerations that forbid us to reject the notion of human nature. Rigorously objective and scientific observation also obliges us to recognize that there exists in all men certain specifically common characteristics that enables naturalists to discern the evidence of a certain evolution. It is certainly not easy to make an inventory of these specific characteristics. But in any case we should strenuously refuse to exhibit the pride of identifying human nature with our own nature. Our nature is only one of the many possible realizations of human nature and nothing authorizes us to consider it the most perfect or final realization.

When paleontologists prove that certain remains that have been discovered by excavation belong to primitive men rather than primates we should not conclude that the former represent a higher degree of biological evolution. On the contrary, we know that some primates were biologically superior to many of our human ancestors. What enables us to identify man are the nonequivocal signs of creativity, invention, and a break with the *established order* of nature. Paleontological evidence can be complemented with that of other anthropological sciences to indicate provisorily that human nature can be defined by its capacity for reflection, creative work, meaningful discourse, and morality. We say by its *capacity* for reflective intelligence, language, freedom, and so forth were not in the beginning given realities but potentialities that were to be actualized by a long and slow process of human maturation, both collective and individual.

It would be false, however, to say that human nature can be defined uniquely by its original potentialities. Just as it is unacceptable to identify the European man of the twentieth century with human nature as such so too is the reduction of human nature to what ethnologists observe in our less evolved ancestors. Rousseau's idealization of the *primitive,* the *good savage,* cannot be scientifically supported. In order for man to be truly man, that is to say in order that he live in perfect conformity with his nature, he must not be stripped of all that centuries of evolution and civilization have added to what we can observe in primitive man. The most specifically human characteristic consists precisely in the impossibility of conceiving the nature of man as static. Either human nature is dynamic and dialectic or there is no human nature.

The nature of Western man today contains all the possibilities that paleontologists have discovered in our distant ancestors. But the innumerable conquests of civilization are by no means foreign additions to our true nature; they are integral to this nature and have become authentic constituent elements. Our nature is therefore very different from that of the Peking or Neanderthal man. Even today human nature is different or, more exactly, differently actualized, depending upon civilizations, cultural evolution, and different collective and individual situations.

There is no reason to think that human nature has attained its highest degree of actualization in the most morally and intellectually evolved men of our time. We share totally Teilhard de Chardin's opinion that the noosphere is presently only at the first stage of its growth. Those who will inhabit our planet one hundred thousand years from now will be at least as different from us as we are from the Neanderthal man. It is difficult to imagine what limits can be set to the growth of the noosphere; we cannot imagine the richness and complexity of human nature in its state of perfection. But we must take one fact as axiomatic: we must look for human nature more in the future than in the past. And to do this we must try to discover the general direction of human evolution. In observing the principal cycles of evolution in the past we note that it was never in an anarchical fashion, at the whim of circumstances that human nature realized its potentialities; an *intention* has always guided this development and it matters little whether this intention was immanent or transcendent to nature. We ought therefore suppose that the same intentionality will continue its work in the centuries to come.

It is in man's nature to transcend continually or attempt to transcend his natural condition—not to free himself completely from nature but to acquire a new natural condition. We in no way destroy the notion of nature to see it as a dynamic and dialectical development. The solidity of what is static is only too apparent. Contrary to the postulates of a certain *philosophy of being*, there is more being, more reality in movement than in rest. It is because it evolves and grows that human nature is becoming richer and more and more complex. There is incontestably an identity between primitive man and the evolved man of today. And while the points of comparison may be few in number, restricted almost entirely to fundamental potentialities, the identity is clear enough to permit us to speak of a humanity that is one and indivisible.

What can we legitimately predict about man's future evolution by observing the principal cycles of his past evolution? Such a prediction is highly relevant to a definition of natural morality.

It is clear, in the first place, that humanity is tending toward greater self-consciousness. The attempt of a certain rationalism of the nineteenth century, which still prevails in some circles, to deny the special reality of the noosphere and thus reduce man to animality has totally failed. The most eminent biologists and anthropologists of our time, whatever be their metaphysical presuppositions, certainly recognize the continuity between the biosphere and the noosphere, the former having been a preparation for the latter but the latter always rooted in the former. There can now be no doubt about the specific nature, the radical novelty of the noosphere. Our increasingly intense awareness of this fact goes hand in hand with the progressive deployment of the potentialities of the noosphere.

In the course of its development human nature has increasingly affirmed its transcendence, its independence with respect to all kinds of determinism. We have no reason to suppose that this liberty will one day become total, but the possibilities of freedom are still infinite. It is probable that in a few generations from now men will depend much less than they do now upon the land for their food and their mobility will no longer be restricted by the boundaries of this world. It is likely, however, that they will become dependent upon something else and limited by other boundaries.

In the past, human creativity found its principal stimulus, and in the beginning its only stimulus, in the necessity of satisfying the elementary needs of life. Today a large part of this creativity is expended to satisfy the needs of the spirit. We can predict that this will be still more the case in the future.

Another constant of human development is a greater and greater unity, both extensively and intensively. Scarcely a half century ago many sociologists noted this tendency and concluded that in a perhaps not too distant future individual consciousness would be totally absorbed. They advocated the collectivization not only of economic goods but also of the most specifically human goods. There would be no lasting love between one man and one woman, the children would have no parents but would be the progeny of the collectivity, and so forth. Since they thought that true human nature was to be sought in the past rather than in the future they argued, on the basis of very slight scientific evidence, that the primitive human consciousness was gregarious, that the affirmation of individual awareness was the result of an antinatural civilization and that a return to the *natural* state was mandatory. That the Marxists understood this return *dialectically* does not detract much from the monumental error of those days which are still so close to us.

We also believe that individualism was a sickness of civilization; but it was a sickness of growth. Before the present phase of human unification began it was probably necessary that men go through a period of extreme abusive awareness of their individuality. It is true that this phase seriously compromised the movement toward unity; but it is also true that all the anti-individualist reactions were salutary. But the renewed movement toward unity must not be explained in terms of a return to an imagined gregarious consciousness in primitive man. Mature human consciousness will be both communal and personal; it will reject both the philosophy of the social contract and that of gregarious collectivism. Here again Teilhard de Chardin has assessed the situation accurately and with great foresight. The kind of socialism he recommended, and which certain African political leaders hope to realize, is quite unlike either Rousseau's individualism or the communism of Marx and Lenin. It seems to us that Chardin's concept of a personalist socialization is directly in line with the growth of human nature, insofar at least as such a line can be discerned at present.

This rather lengthy analysis of human nature is quite in keeping with the subject of the present chapter. Natural morality must be a morality that conforms to the nature of man. If our conception of human nature is correct then the task of natural morality is not the conservation of an established order of social or individual values. Current morality, whether Christian or lay, is radically conservative. I don't think we ought to blame this state of affairs on the hypocrisy of those who have vested interests in the present order. It is interesting to note that Marxist morality, which claimed to be a substitute for conservative bourgeois morality, itself became conservative as soon as its adherents were solidly established in power. In 1925 the morality professed in Soviet Russia was just the opposite of bourgeois morality in matters of the family, work, property, patriotism, internationalism, and the like; today the differences between the two moralities are scarcely discernible. This is because both the bourgeois and the communists see human nature as something static; quite logically natural morality will be in the service of human nature as one conceives it.

Human nature, we have said, is to be sought more in the future than in the past. Consequently natural morality ought to be less concerned with the conservation of the past than with building the future. In this sense all authentic morality is necessarily *revolutionary*, on the condition, evidently, that the word *revolution* is understood dialectically, the emphasis being put not upon the upsetting and destruction of what is but upon the creation of what must be. As soon as morality becomes conservative, that is to say static, it ceases to be *natural*. Contrary to the hopes placed in it, it becomes inefficacious, incapable even of preserving from decadence and destruction what is authentically natural in the moral values of the past. Obviously it is in no position to promote the natural values of the humanity of tomorrow.

Some of the *great principles* of natural morality are effectively immutable, indeed one might say eternal: generosity, justice, respect for human dignity, liberty, equality, respect for parents and old people, freedom, honesty, sincerity, purity, and others. But the analysis of such principles is not enough to define natural morality any more than an analysis of the fundamental potentialities of man is sufficient to define human nature. Potentialities must be actualized; moral principles must be concretized in terms of the degree of maturity attained by human nature. Some primitive tribes considered eating the remains of their parents the highest form of respect, while we consider it the height of immorality. There can be little doubt that our way of honoring our parents is more in keeping with natural morality than that of primitive man for the simple reason that we are in a position to presume that the potentialities of human nature are more fully actualized in us than in, say, a given tribe of New Guinea.

The French Republic proclaims on all its official buildings the fraternity, liberty, and equality of all of its citizens. We think this is one of the cardinal principles of natural morality. But what kind of concrete equality does it oblige us to promote? Is it enough that all are equal before the law? Does it imply an equality of opportunity? Or must we go further, with the utopian socialists of yesteryear, and proclaim that only absolute equality of goods and standard of living conforms to natural morality? Must we hope, with Lenin, that in the future communist society all men will be equal in genius, beauty, and strength? It is evident that there is no easy answer to such questions. The kind of equality we consider natural today seemed immoral centuries ago and it is quite likely that what will be considered equality in centuries to come passes our imagination. The same is true of freedom and of all other *eternal* moral values.

On the level of clear ideas that are so attractive to pure reason our conception of natural morality is less satisfying than the classical static conception. To succeed in establishing that only private property—or collective property—only monarchy or democracy, only monogamy or only free love conform to natural morality would be a simplification, perhaps comforting but false, of human existence. The greater part of the most difficult problems would have a ready-made solution that could be presented to or forced upon men. The difference between morality and the law would practically disappear since morality would then become simply the law interiorized. The moral progress of individuals and social groups would be measured by their greater or less conformity to a moral law, a law that would be considered immutable in all of its details. The partisans, still numerous in our day, of this conception of natural morality cry scandal as soon as one dares speak not only of moral progress but also of the progress of morality.

Unfortunately, *clear ideas,* in this domain as in others, prove to be poor and simplistic ideas that do not embrace the complexity of reality. I am aware that to admit the evolutionary character of natural morality would force moralists periodically to reassess human nature and consequently more or less important revisions of natural morality would have to be undertaken. No one will deny that this involves risks. Some spiritually immature persons will undoubtedly object that since good and evil today are not quite the good and evil of the past and that the good and evil of the future will be different than those of today, moral obligation has no foundation in the *nature of things,* that each is then free to define his own morality. But does there exist a single domain of human existence that has attained a certain degree of authenticity from which all risk of error and false interpretation could be excluded? A refusal to recognize the evolutionary character of human nature and natural morality would perhaps make it impossible for some people of bad faith to claim exemption from moral obligation; but the facts are there to show that the immutability of principles scarcely promote morality. Morality is not a speculative science whose end is to know eternal essences. It is a practical discipline whose purpose is to regulate the conduct of men *hic et nunc.*

Let us make ourselves clear: in rejecting the notion of a static and immutable human nature, a kind of incarnation of the Platonic, eternal ideal of man, we are not therefore adopting the theories of those sociologists who identify morality with the science of mores. The latter, let us insist once more, can be of great help to the moralists; but its purpose is merely to take an inventory of a given state of customs in a given society of a given period. A morality based on this science would approve as moral behavior what was in accordance with these customs and disapprove as immoral behavior what departed from them. Thus specialists in the science of customs, having observed that adultery is common among men in France today, would conclude that it is moral while adultery on the part of the woman, since it is generally disapproved by current mores, would be immoral. Likewise fiscal fraud and other forms of theft from the state would be tolerated by the French but severely condemned by the English. Morality, in this matter at least, would change depending upon which side of the English channel is considered. Much worse, every reaction against the reigning mores, in all logic, would be immoral. The evolution of morality would be predicated upon a prior change in customs.

A morality founded upon the science of mores would not merit the name of morality. All morality is by definition normative. It has the further purpose, as we have said, not of conserving a given state of mores or of human nature, but of developing them. Those mores which are consonant with the growth of human nature are moral and ought to be protected and developed by morality. Other mores, however embedded or generalized they be, are clearly contrary to the nature of the noosphere and ought consequently to be rejected by natural morality. There is a third group of customs that are morally neutral, neither favoring nor interfering with the deployment of the noosphere.

Only a dynamic conception of human nature and natural

morality can foster the reformatory—and even revolutionary—action of those who are courageous enough to enter the battle against the established moral order and become founders of a new morality. We are thinking of such figures as Confucius and Socrates, Francis of Assisi and Gandhi. We are thinking especially of the profound moral revolution introduced by Christ. Those who refuse to understand the dynamic character of natural morality argue that Christ reestablished this natural morality in its pristine dignity. Now that is from an historical point of view absolutely false. No one had ever lived according to the Beatitudes. Christ's morality is not then the reestablishment of an ancient morality that had been corrupted by sin, but a veritable new morality. It is not for this reason less a *natural morality*. It is eminently so because more than any other, it has enabled human nature to reach a new level of growth.

CHAPTER 7

The Universality of the
Moral Law

THE MORAL law presents itself to each of us as an obligation to do good and avoid evil. Its particularity consists in this that the obligation is not imposed upon us from the outside by social authority but from within by our conscience. When our conscience does not guide our behavior, when we do good and avoid evil only because we are constrained to do so by external authority, then properly speaking we are *amoral*.

In order that the imperatives of the moral law appear to everyone as categorical, that is to say as unconditionally obligatory, it is important that men be convinced of the universality of the moral law. This is easy in closed societies where it is understood that our own conception of good and evil is the only valid one. But civilization today cannot make do with this simple and simplistic vision. To be sure modern civilization is convinced of the necessity of a universal moral obligation; but when it is a question of knowing the concrete content of good and evil and the subject matter of moral obligation, difficulties are inevitable.

Descartes, who in this was quite faithful to medieval philosophy, thought that it was *sufficient to judge correctly to act rightly*. Good and evil in this view were construed as objective realities which could be recognized as such. The logical consequences of this premise leads to an approval of the Platonic thesis that we sin only by ignorance, that ignorance is the sole cause of evil. Christian rationalists tempered this view somewhat by admitting the perversity of the will; indeed they saw in this faculty the principal cause of the reason's inability to discern good and evil.

The nineteenth century and first decades of the twentieth century, under the convergent influence of Rousseau and Kant, broke with the ancient and Cartesian objectivism. Good and evil and therefore moral obligation are not to be sought in exterior things but in the heart of each of us. For morality to triumph, the inward eye of each individual must become sincere and pure.

We also believe that the moral law is inscribed in man's conscience, that this is the criterion of good and evil. But unlike the subjectivism of Rousseau or Kant we are of the opinion that the conscience that dictates our behavior is neither rigorously individual nor absolutely infallible. Individual conscience must be in intimate communication with the social conscience since moral good and evil are as much, if not more, social realities as they are individual. The moral law, too, is as much social as it is individual. We are firmly opposed to the thesis, held in the past by many philosophers and moralists, that it is sufficient that each person pursue his own good. The hope that the common good would be thereby promoted in an indirect way is fallacious. Society is not a juxtaposition of individual egoisms but a community whose members are integral parts. It follows that moral obligation is inseparably individual and collective, that we ought to pursue the common good and personal good in the same moral movement.

It is evident that, in the past, the necessary universality of the moral law was illusory. The social group with which the individual identified and whose good he willed was so restricted that there could be no question of universality. Modern subjectivism, which is the negation of a truly universal moral law, is the direct consequence of modern man's empirical awareness of the infinite diversity of moral obligations in ancient societies as well as in those of today.

Yet, as we have insisted, the moral law would lose much of its efficacy if it ceased to be considered as universal. We do not have to resort to artificial arguments to establish this universality; it is intrinsic to *the nature of things*. To understand it, let us recall what we said in earlier chapters to the effect that the true image of human nature, and therefore of an authentic natural morality, is to be sought in the future rather than the past.

Civilized men of our time are aware of themselves not as members of a clan or a tribe but of infinitely more vast societies. Perhaps the average man thinks of himself as belonging to a nation or a class. But large numbers have already transcended these limitations; for them the only authentic community is mankind in its totality. For such men the moral law is truly universal not only in the sense that the good toward which they tend and the evil they combat are conceived as the good and evil of all men, but further because they conceive the moral obligation in the same manner, independently of their religion. There are magnificent pages in the writings of such varied authors as Teilhard de Chardin, Bertrand Russell, Einstein, Bergson, and other eminent representatives of modern man that eloquently attest to the universality of their moral conscience.

We have no reason to fear that the evolutionary character of human nature and morality endangers the universality of the moral law. Quite the contrary, everything leads us to hope that what is the case for an elite today will be true for the great majority of men tomorrow. More and more rapid means of communication, larger political and economic unions, the cosmopolitan character of culture as a result of mass media are all instruments in the service of an authentically universal consciousness.

In the name of the universality of the moral law European colonizers of former times sought to impose upon foreign peoples their own ideas with regard to marriage, property, work and so forth. What generally resulted was a serious compromise of fundamental human rights and sometimes even the destruction of important moral values. This was because the human nature of the Peruvians, the Chinese or the Congolese was very differently concretized from that of the Spanish, English or French. But, as we shall have occasion to note in more detail in the second part of this book, the elaboration of an almost universal morality is already possible in our day. Thus, for example, almost all peoples, at least in their elite, are aware of the dignity of the human person as such and, as a result of this, their moral conscience no longer tolerates either slavery or marriage by abduction or barter. Likewise in the matter of private property the ancient quarrel between the partisans of private property and the partisans of collective property is well on the way to becoming anachronistic. Even in those states that most explicitly profess the *mystique* of free enterprise the rights of others as persons is recognized. Pope John XXIII himself has advocated the socialization of riches, a thesis which formerly was defended in Christian circles only by liberals who were considered heretics by their coreligionists.

The mechanism of the evolutionary process is not in itself a sufficient guarantee of the universality of the moral law in the minds of all men. Within the perspective of the noosphere such mechanisms never operate infallibly. Men, especially those of the elite, ought to deliberately give themselves to the task of transcending present limitations and urge the masses to place their liberty in the service of the same transcendence. We therefore do not regret the "good old days" when life was lived under the illusion of the *given* universality of the moral law, but we enthusiastically take up the challenge of realizing ourselves.

CHAPTER 8

The Two Moralities

Nietzsche, probably inspired by St. Paul's reference to the slaves who lived under the Law and the children of God who were free, formulated his all too famous theory of two moralities —the master morality and the slave morality. It goes without saying that this theory is far from what St. Paul intended. The *slaves,* that is to say the generality of men, must, according to the German philosopher, strictly observe the prescriptions of current morality and society has the right to impose it upon them by physical constraint if necessary. The *masters,* or *supermen,* are bound by no objective moral law. Whatever they do is good by definition; what they reject can only be evil. Some of Nietzsche's disciples went to extremes in applying these principles practically. The Nazis extended the master-slave principle to nations. The *master race,* that is to say the German people, acted morally in exterminating Jewish and Polish people and imposing its yoke on numerous other nations. The unconditional duty of the slave peoples was to submit to the law imposed upon them by the masters.

Despite the brutal lesson history has drawn from the Nazi adventure, Nietzsche's theory still has its partisans. Obviously those who profess it consider themselves masters and thus able to put themselves above the moral law. Often they are the only ones to recognize their superiority to the common run of slaves whom they despise and over whom they try to exercise their *will to power.*

Bergson's distinction between open and closed morality is a more legitimate one. The psychoanalyst Charles Odier also speaks of *two sources of morality*. The first of these is unconscious, the second conscious. Odier's theory has some truth in it but his position, in spite of the similarity of terminology, is much different from Bergson's. The latter did not hold that closed morality originated uniquely in the unconscious; it is far from being the only product of what Freud called the *superego*. Bergson did not seem to be familiar with that term, so dear to psychoanalysts. In any case, the sources of closed morality are conscious as well as unconscious. Bergson's notion is somewhat parallel to what Christian moralists call a *morality of fear*. Some of its interdictions or imperatives have their source in ancient taboos, embedded deeply in the unconscious; others result from the constraints imposed upon individuals by the family, the state, or the Church. One is always constrained, whether interiorly or exteriorly, to submit to the dictates of closed morality. Such a morality is evidently incapable of promoting personal or collective existence; it creates no values; yet it is far from being condemnable. Most of the members of primitive societies as well as a good number of members of evolved societies are incapable of acting morally unless they are constrained to do so. If the precepts of a closed morality did not govern their conduct they would have to be imprisoned or kept under constant surveillance to prevent them from harming themselves and others. But in this case behavior is only objectively moral for from a subjective point of view freedom is scarcely involved at the stage of closed morality; and, as we noted earlier, only a free act can be called moral in the proper sense of the term.

A superior, and the only authentic morality, is *open morality*. Those who act under its guidance do good and avoid evil not because they are obliged to, nor from hope of reward or fear of punishment; they act out of pure generosity or, to use a more Christian term, out of charity. *"Love and do what you will,"* said St. Augustine. True love wills only the good. He who follows a morality of love is like the follower of Nietzsche's master morality in the sense that for both the good is what they will. But the respective motor forces of love and the will to power are fundamentally heterogeneous. Nietzsche's master is thinking of himself, of the exaltation of his will to power. The morality of love tends toward others, toward a transcendent ideal. For the latter the objectivity of the moral law is in no way abolished, but it is interiorized to the point where the objective and the subjective coincide perfectly.

From a psychological point of view we can say that there is no obligation, in the strict sense of the term, in open morality. I know a scholar, a fervent Christian, who dedicated his whole life to the altruistic service of others. He was profoundly shocked when a priest told him that he would be rewarded in heaven for the good he did on earth; he had never thought about reward. It is a common opinion among non-Christian thinkers that open morality, as Bergson describes it, is not possible for Christians since they must always act in the hope of recompense in the next life. Teilhard de Chardin and a good number of other Christians who are committed to the improvement of humanity categorically reject the idea of a commerce between the believer and his God in terms of which the former would give himself fully to the task of being a man only because he was promised eternal life. The hope of such a reward plays a great role in closed morality for it is a fact that the majority of Christians are far from the perspectives of open morality. Those who practice an open morality, and there are far more Christians who do so than is commonly suspected, practically never think of reward. They evidently believe in and hope for eternal life but this is not a result of their efforts but of a free gift of God. For their part, they imitate God by acting out of altruistic motives.

Bergson was therefore right. In point of fact there are two moralities which, in their essence, are qualitatively heterogeneous. Psychologically, from the point of view of the moral subject, the abyss that separates the two is much less difficult to bridge than Bergson's rhapsodic descriptions of open morality would lead one to believe. Probably only the saints of different religions live the open morality fully. But it does not follow that all others remain imprisoned in closed morality which has its origin in the superego, taboos, social conventions, the hope of rewards, and the fear of punishment in the next life. When we look closely we see that there is something altruistic and generous in the behavior of the most primitive man. Ordinarily his actions are guided by closed morality; however, from time to time the spark of generosity flashes forth. Little by little, as we progressively enter the noosphere, this spark becomes a flame, a flame that can increase indefinitely. Depth psychologists can discern in the psyche of almost all those whose moral authenticity we admire most remnants of closed morality. It follows that open morality is less a given than a never ending conquest. At bottom it is evolutionary and follows the same laws of growth and maturation as man himself and mankind at large.

I remember the astonishment on the part of the chaplain, lawyer, and warden of a young man condemned to death. While in prison he conducted himself toward all those he contacted with such generosity that he won the admiration and sympathy of all, to the point that they found it incredible that a man of such exceptional moral caliber could be executed. There is always the possibility, of course, that the young criminal underwent a genuine conversion. But it is not psychologically unlikely that his generosity coexisted in him with perverse tendencies, tendencies which could only have been controlled by the constraints of closed morality which were not effective in his case.

Only the psychically mature man is capable of leading an authentically open moral life. Only he can victoriously confront the anarchical drive of his instincts and the temptations of the world around him. While closed morality is legalistic and applies the automatic rules to ready-made situations, open morality is inventive and creative, a perpetual questioning of what one has acquired.

Open morality, and it is important to insist upon this point, is not the privilege of saints alone. There are undoubtedly many unbelievers who are sufficiently mature to live according to the unwritten laws of open morality. On the other hand, while evangelical morality is in our opinion the highest form of open morality, the majority of Christians remain at the level of closed morality. It seems further that many of the saints, unless their biographers have done them an injustice, were not free of the legalism of closed morality, that the fear of transgressing the letter of the law was as strong in them as generosity.

Effectively, closed morality demands respect for the letter of the law: the law is the law! Such a morality is understandably a convenient one for those who are psychologically immature—whether they be primitives, adolescents, or neurotics. Not being able to assume entire responsibility for their actions, they are at peace with their conscience when they have obeyed the letter of the law.

Open morality, motivated by charity or generosity, does not necessarily demand more than closed morality, but it demands it differently. It demands the commitment rather than the submission of freedom. Its adherents could, in certain circumstances, deliberately transgress the letter of the moral law if they were convinced that in respecting it they would betray the spirit of the law. However moving we find Socrates' choosing obedience to the laws of his country over liberty and life, our admiration for the Greek sage would not be diminished if he had taken advantage of the opportunity offered him to escape from prison. He would have thus clearly disobeyed the written law of his country but not necessarily its spirit since from all evidence the political leaders were in this case at fault. During the Second World War man's inhumanity to man became painfully clear. It is probable that the executioners of the extermination camps never posed the question of their personal responsibility. Their psychic immaturity would not have enabled them to do so. Under the dominion of a closed morality, their conscience was at peace because they obeyed. Nor can we doubt the sincerity of those war criminals who expressed such astonishment when they were called upon to give an account of their crimes. They were being judged in terms of a morality of freedom and generosity which was not their morality. The same is true of the soldier of the Foreign Legion whom the French courts condemned to death for the assassination of a lawyer sympathetic to the Algerian cause. His superiors had ordered the assassination and his deformed conscience would have been ill at ease had he disobeyed them.

We touch here upon one of the essential components of the present moral crisis. The degree of evolution reached by modern civilization is no longer reconcilable with closed morality. But too many individuals and groups are too psychically immature to accept their liberty, to love a humanity that is one and indivisible. They can only love one country in opposition to another and they are only too glad to hand over their liberty and responsibility to some providential leader.

We clearly have every right to expect that the accelerated rhythm of the growth of the noosphere will permit an increasing number of men to attain the maturity indispensable to the practice of a morality of love. Yet it remains true that probably for some time to come a closed morality of fear and constraint will be necessary to mankind in general. The beautiful anarchy that many generous hearts dreamed of, especially in the last century, is not about to become a reality tomorrow. It is symptomatic that the word *anarchy* evokes for most men the idea of disorder and chaos, of bombings and hold ups, while in the minds of those optimists who were the theoreticians of anarchy, the inutility of all government and all constraint seemed a necessary result of the rapid accession of all men to a morality of love.

However imperfect and inauthentic closed morality seems to us it would be a serious mistake to want to abolish it prematurely. The criticisms levelled against psychoanalysis in this respect are not without justification. Abusively identifying social morality, which in Bergson's language, we call closed morality, with the famous superego exercising tyrannical control over the unconscious, some Freudians think that the first task of psychoanalysis is to liberate the subject from all moral constraints. Even supposing that the superego were as dangerous as they say it is, it still seems to me indispensable as long as man is not yet ready for a morality of liberty and love. The great superiority of that other form of depth psychology, namely psychosynthesis, lies precisely in this that it is not content to liberate the subject from unconscious constraints but endeavors to lead him to a higher level of spiritual existence. When one is capable of living an open morality of love, closed morality will cease to exercise its constraints upon him.

The appointed guardians of morality and the moral order wrongly see in the theory of two moralities a danger for morality as such. It is rather their ignorance of this fact that is dangerous and could be catastrophic. To preach the morality of free and mature men to children or, what comes to the same thing, to those who are adult by age but not emotionally, far from promoting a superior level of existence, would likely discourage them or encourage total amorality. To paraphrase St. Paul the meat of adults is not suitable for children.

Equally dangerous is the pretension to nourish adults with baby food under the pretext that it is good for children. Well-intentioned people frequently tell us: "We do not deny the legitimacy, even the necessity, of an open morality for adults. But don't you ever think of the harm your theories might do to the immature and simple?" They admit that these things might be talked about in private but should not be bruited abroad in books and articles that are accessible to all. We do not deny the possibility of this danger. But we think a greater danger is courted by men and women who have become psychically mature without a corresponding morality, one adapted to their level of development and their needs. It is particularly agonizing that Christian intellectuals do not have a morality capable of guiding them in their scientific or sociological researches. Thus, for example, it is a fact that problems so important for the future of mankind as those of war and peace are debated by statesmen almost completely outside any authentically moral consideration. Could this not be at least partially the fault of those moralists who have failed to confront problems at this level? All treatises of morality have, to be sure, a chapter on war and peace; but what is said in them is scarcely related to anything going on in the real world. In any case, the problem is never discussed in the perspective of an authentically open morality, which alone is capable of leading to an adequate solution. Or, to take another example, more individual this time, a sexual morality founded on interdictions can be useful to someone who is emotionally immature. If, however, it is imposed upon the emotionally mature it could only have negative results. Only a sexual morality founded upon love can be satisfactory.

CHAPTER 9

Morality With or Without Sin?

The ill-tempered hostility of Freud and many of his disciples toward morality and in particular Christian morality is well known. Not that they thought rules of conduct and the distinction between good and evil harmful or superfluous. But this, they held, was not the essence of morality. Morality for them is intrinsically bound up with the idea of sin and it is this that is fundamentally objectionable. The morality of sin is the principal cause of neurosis; further, it is an obstacle to the purpose of human existence, namely the pursuit of happiness. Some years ago the French Freudian, Hesnard, devoted two important works to a critique of the morality of sin which he proposed to replace with an ethics without sin.

What conception, then, do the Freudians have of sin? It is not so much an evil as an *evil within the individual*. Freud's explanation of the origin of sin is a psychoanalytic accommodation of the ancient Greek legend of Oedipus and the Judeo-Christian teaching on original sin. The latter, according to the biblical narrative and theological doctrine, consisted in a rupture of a primitive state of innocence by the common ancestor of all men who disobeyed God in eating of the fruit of the tree of good and evil. Whence the penchant for evil in the heart of all human beings; whence, too, the guilt feelings that everyone experiences even when they are conscious of no personal moral fault. Thus man was henceforward established in a state of sin which the redemption of Christ enabled him to overcome. For Freud the biblical narrative is a mere legend which gives a poor account of the tormenting guilt that darkens the joy of living. We have given an account of his Oedipus theory in an earlier chapter.

In an earlier work, *The Psychology of Loving,* we analyzed more in depth Freud's hypothesis and found its principal weakness to be a total lack of historical foundation, a purely imaginary projection. In any event, Freud considers morality's prohibition of incest as the cruellest mutilation that has in the course of time been imposed upon the love life of men. And since for him all of morality originates in the Oedipus complex he therefore condemns the morality of sin as such and assigns psychoanalysis the task of abolishing it.

Dr. Hesnard is much less inclined than his master to fabricate legends. Yet he is not less categorical in his condemnation of a morality of sin. Since sin is defined as a purely interior guilt, a morality that has as its primary goal the avoidance of sin turns man in upon himself. The purity of intentions, in this perspective, is much more important than the purity of actions. This accounts for man's social inefficacy and his predisposition to neurosis. Moreover, to liberate himself from guilt feelings that have no precise object the subject sometimes has recourse to actions that are objectively blameworthy. Thus most sex crimes are committed by those who are sexually *repressed* and many assassinations are the work of timid souls who, generally as a result of a too effeminate education, have repressed their aggressivity.

Hesnard advocates a morality animated exclusively by an altruistic ideal. Man ought to do good not to alleviate his guilt feelings but because he loves others and wishes them well. Thus, to take an example, sexual acts would have moral content only from the point of view of their social consequences; what relates to personal sexuality pertains not to morality but solely to hygiene.

We have no objection to an ethics that is altruistically inspired. But the adverb "exclusively" could cause misunderstandings. In the preceding chapters we tried to establish the conditions of a morality that would intensify the quality of life not only among the few but with the generality of men. With Hesnard we do not think that moral value resides essentially in what curbs man's natural impulses but rather in harmonious relations with others. It is, moreover, a serious psychological mistake to suppose that man's natural impulses are always evil ones, orientated toward egoistical pleasures. Pessimistic moralists like Pascal, La Roche-foucauld, and to some extent perhaps St. Paul and St. Augustine all misunderstood the essentially evolutionary character of human nature. We have already noted that even in the most corrupt of men very generous natural impulses are to be found. And clinical experience teaches us that egoism and asociability are often more or less neurotic deviations of naturally altruistic impulses.

Freud, Hesnard and many other psychoanalysts have a very false idea of sin. They wrongly identify it with the irrational and unconscious taboos whose devastating consequences they observe in their psychopathic patients. The psychopath is in fact eaten by an interior anguish of guilt without being able to say just what he is guilty of. He is trying to shake off his guilt feelings more than any specific sin. He is more concerned with intentions than actions. This has nothing to do with the morality of sin; the proof of this is that this kind of psychopath is encountered among nonbelievers, who have no sense of sin, just as often as among believers.

The notion of sin in the higher religions, and particularly in Christianity, has nothing in common with corrosive guilt feelings. They conceive sin not as a purely interior culpability but as a specific failure to observe the moral law which is considered the expression of the divine will. Most of those who adhere to the morality of sin certainly do not exaggerate in the direction of interiorization. They might rather be accused of an excessive moral legalism. Moralists endeavor to determine precisely what is and what is not a sin, as well as the degree of gravity of each sin. I was astonished to read recently in a manual of moral theol ogy that is used in seminaries long developments on the morality of kissing between engaged couples. There were minute distinctions between legitimate kisses, those which constituted a venial sin and those which were mortal. It was in reacting against this kind of moral legalism that Pascal and others stressed the intention of the moral agent and tried to interiorize morality. Of course, as Hesnard himself admits, it is evident that every morality has some interior dimension.

As a reaction against the excessive materialization of morality there was a swing toward the opposite excess. Because the intention is an essential element of a moral act, some spiritual writers concluded that it was enough to have good intentions, that the objective content of actions had little importance before God. This kind of interiorization obviously fosters scruples in those who are inclined to neurosis. Whatever the scrupulous person does he is forever worried about his intentions. It is understandable that some psychotherapists have little respect for this kind of morality and indeed consider it altogether undesirable.

Authentic morality ought to be less a barrier against evil than an instrument of good. If preachers and other guardians of morality generally stress the negative dimension it is not usually for theoretical reasons but because they feel called upon to deliver some immediate remedy. By threatening their congregations with punishment, they hope to protect the collectivity from their evil inclinations. The psychologist must disagree with this approach; it is far healthier to give people a taste for the good, to liberate their good natural impulses from what impedes their expression. But this is another matter not directly connected with the objections made against a morality of sin.

Those who make such objections seem to overlook the fact that the morality of sin is far from being purely negative. Thus the Catholic confesses, in the *Confiteor*, not only the evil that he has done but also the good which he has not done, his *sins of omission*. The emphasis upon the first of these is largely due to a widespread influence of Jansenism and explains why unbelievers like Freud formulated erroneous ideas of sin. It is a happy sign that preaching today is accentuating more and more the positive aspect of the moral function.

Thus a morality of sin does not have as its purpose the cultivation of guilt feelings. Like any morality it is engaged in the enterprise of making men develop their sense of responsibility. What distinguishes morality with sin from morality without sin is that in the latter man is responsible only before others while in the former he is also responsible before his Creator. Sin is a specifically religious notion. Guilt is largely a psychological matter.

On the other hand, the religious man who is psychologically mature gives sin a minor role in motivating his personal moral behavior. Objectively he admits that sin forms an integral part of morality, it is displeasing to God and one tries to avoid it. But one acts morally neither out of fear of punishment nor hope of reward but uniquely out of natural generosity and love of God. Usually such a person does not distinguish the two sources; the love of God enlightens and elevates his natural generosity and the two form a unified motive. The truly religious man is not much concerned with the purity of his intentions. His morality, like all authentic morality, is a morality of action.

Two of my friends, both talented writers, disagree as to the usefulness of the idea of sin for moral life. Both live what Bergson would call an open morality. One, a fervent believer, says that his belief in sin was of great help in his moral ascent, that without it the quality of his life would be different. Not that he acts morally out of fear of hell. He rarely thinks of it. But in the Catholic perspective sin is first of all disobedience to the law of God; since love has primacy in his psyche it is because he does not want to offend One he loves that he avoids sin. The other, an agnostic, has difficulty understanding this position. Since he doesn't believe in God his moral life needs no transcendent reference.

Which of the two is right? Undoubtedly both are since both render a faithful account of their own experience. If one thinks that the idea of sin is necessary for his moral life while the other does not, the difference is undoubtedly due to different psychic structures, to different *temperaments*. Further, the morality of sin as professed by the Catholic writer scarcely resembles what psychoanalysts understand by that term. It emanates from a motive of generosity as much as does the morality without sin of the agnostic writer.

Guided by my experience rather than by any doctrinal postulate, I believe that at a certain level of existential authenticity morality without sin and a morality with sin can be equally efficacious. This was Teilhard de Chardin's opinion. Having worked for many years with scholars of all religions and no religion he observed that respect for human dignity, the love of truth, and the good was not the privilege of any category. Teilhard has been wrongly accused in some Catholic circles of thereby denying the eminent role that religion plays in morality. As no theologian would dare deny that there are saints in the Church as well as in other religions, so one cannot doubt the possibility of high moral lives within a system of different moralities.

The moralist must never forget that superior morality is in any hypothesis a reality with but a small number of people, at least in the present stage of evolution. If we understand sin in a religious sense, a sense substantially different than that recognized by most psychoanalysts, it seems very probable that a morality with sin rather than a morality without sin is more effective in promoting moral good—whether the latter be understood in a social or individual sense. If we agree that the first end of morality is not to promote the interior perfection of individuals but their social coexistence it would then be evident that those who avoid evil out of fear of sin have already objectively placed themselves outside the *moral order*. But we must remind ourselves again that the morality of sin includes sins of omission. It follows therefore that it is far from being a purely negative morality. As our examples above illustrated, the idea of sin is not identical with a morality founded upon fear. It can also find a place in a spirituality and a morality inspired by natural generosity and supernatural charity.

If theologians are really convinced that a morality with sin is true not only theoretically but also in the context of social practice, they ought to carefully consider the objections psychology levels against such a morality. Freud, Hesnard, and others are not alone in their negative conception of sin and the morality of sin. It exists in the consciences of many believers and is expressed in many sermons and books. Sin is neither a juridical concept nor a neurotic projection of unconscious taboos; it signifies the reference of human acts to an absolute, to God.

CHAPTER 10

Christian Morality

An EMINENT preacher, in most respects a very educated man, declared in a sermon: "Were it proven to me that Christian revelation is false I would still remain a Christian because of the incontestable superiority of *Christian morality*." He is certainly not the only one to hold this opinion. There are large numbers who do not believe in the dogmas of Christianity but still defend it because they think Christian morality is necessary for them and for others, especially for the education of youth. On the other hand, perhaps more numerous are those who have broken with the Christian faith because Christian morality did not appeal to them or seemed impractical for *ordinary men*. There are also those, mostly spiritual descendents of Nietzsche, who think that Christian morality is not demanding enough and this is a sufficient motive for not believing in Christian dogmas.

As we noted earlier primitive human societies did not distinguish between religion, morality, law, and hygiene. Little by little morality became distinct from law and hygiene; but even today it retains a close connection with religion; indeed it has always appeared inseparable from it. Believers often have difficulty in understanding how atheists and agnostics can be truly moral. And of course lay moralists have tried to set morality on other than religious foundations or they propose to conserve Christian morality, which they judge good, independently of the Christian faith, which they do not share. Yet the simple fact that lay morality resembles Christian morality confirms believers in their conviction that Christian morality is the best of all moralities, that its origin is certainly divine and, consequently, it is blasphemous to speak of its evolution or adaptation. The only reform of morality acceptable to them is a return to the *eternal principles* of Christian morality.

When the partisans—or adversaries—of Christian morality are asked to define what they mean it is usually the morality currently professed, if not practiced, in the West that they have in mind. In addition to the rigorous demands in matters of sex, Christian morality requires respect for private property, the authority of the state, and that of parents. The more demanding also speak of social justice and respect for the life of another. The Catholic social action movement which was very active between the two World Wars endeavored to extend the domain of Christian morality beyond interindividual morality and construct a Christian social doctrine. This view gained authoritative support from a series of pontifical documents and undoubtedly played an important role in the evolution of social ideas in the Christian world. However, we are forced to recognize that, a few general principles excepted, this Christian social doctrine is very vaguely articulated. For many of its spokesmen, including members of the hierarchy, it seems to be principally a matter of *humanizing* existing social relationships. For the Christian avant garde a social morality could not legitimately be called Christian unless almost all the present social structures were seriously questioned. A few of these, for whom morality implies radically revolutionary solutions, feel impelled to collaborate in fact, if not in principle, with the communists.

In our opinion it is quite false to call the current morality of the West Christian. It seems to us especially dangerous to the moral progress of mankind to consider this morality eternal, under the pretext that the revealed truth of Christianity is. There is no de facto proportion between belief in the Trinity, The Incarnation, the Eucharist, or other mysteries of the faith and the concrete forms of relationships between men.

Historically speaking, it is incontestable that Christianity played a preponderant role in the moral formation of the West and, by means of cultural and political influence, upon the modern world as such. So-called Christian morality, however, was not revealed by God as something finished and immutable. It is well known that most of its principles were already formulated in the Old Testament. But we must remind ourselves that the different books of the Old Testament were a result of a slow spiritual maturation on the part of the Jewish people; otherwise we would be hard put to justify the apparent contradictions one can discern within *biblical morality*. Whoever fails to bear in mind the pedagogical character of biblical teaching and considers each word as the expression of an eternal truth cannot but be troubled by the low moral level of many of its requirements. There is no question that the Chinese and even Greek moralists who were contemporaries of Moses and Isaias, had a much higher moral ideal than that presented in the oldest biblical writings just as, for that matter, there is a great difference between these writings and those of the later prophets of Israel.

The Old Testament is by no means the only source of Christian morality. Whether by a special design of providence or simply because of the historical circumstances of the time, it is a fact that Christianity in the beginning took root among the peoples of the Greco-Roman culture. It would have been impossible to abolish the traditional mores, customs, and laws of these peoples. The Apostle Paul understood that just as the Jewish Christian communities had evangelized biblical morality so too those who preached to the Gentiles ought not subject them to the Jewish law but directly evangelize their respective mores, customs, and laws. Later, with the conversion of eminent representatives of the Greco-Roman culture, the positive contributions of this culture to Christian morality became greater and even preponderant. Without compromising the deposit of biblical morality Origen, Clement of Alexandria, the Gregories, Basil, and other Church Fathers drew consciously, and perhaps more so unconsciously, from the moral teaching of Socrates and Plato, the Stoics, and other sages of the ancient world while in the Middle Ages Aquinas baptized the ethics of Aristotle.

Later, when Christianity spread to France and Germany, a similar syncretism took place. The Christians condemned some elements of these cultures, modified others, and found still others quite to their taste. As with ancient culture, Christian morality both modified the new cultures and was modified by them. We personally regret that this same flexibility did not prevail in later missionary efforts in the Far East and Africa. By the time Christianity began to evangelize these cultures Christian morality had become too codified to permit a similar osmosis with what was best in the moral traditions of the countries in question. The cause of Christian universality is certainly the worse for this failure.

But we can still with good reason speak of a *Christian morality*. In it the relationship between the specifically evangelical content and the contribution of different cultures is comparable to the traditional relationship between the supernatural and the natural. The supernatural does not abolish the natural but elevates it to a qualitatively superior level. Likewise Christian morality does not abolish natural moralities but transfigures them qualitatively. Now, as we have stated in our previous analyses, human nature is less a gift than a task, less to be sought in the past than in the future. This being the case, morality, in order to promote the human nature of the future, ought not become wedded to the dated values of the past but be always a little in advance of the present stage of the evolution of the noosphere. Origen in the third century, Ambrose and Augustine in the fifth and sixth centuries, Francis of Assisi, and Thomas Aquinas in the thirteenth century were profoundly aware of the realities of their own time but were also precursors of time to come. It was for this reason that the Christian morality they taught proved to be marvelously effective. Christian morality lost its efficacy when its protagonists failed to recognize the evolutionary character of human reality. Not adjusting to present reality, by that token it failed to anticipate future reality.

Must we conclude from the foregoing considerations that morality ought to assert its independence of religion as it formerly did from civil law and hygiene? There is no doubt that a too narrow identification of religion with a given morality harms religion. Religion is the bearer of eternal truths; only their formulation is susceptible to modifications with the passage of time. But morality implies far more fundamental transformations. Because, for example, a given form of property or government has in the past been justified in the name of Christian morality, those whose sociological or political convictions lead them to believe in some other form of property or government were at the same time led to believe that the religion which supported dated social and political structures was also dated. Many proletariats believed they had to break with the Christian faith because they were socialists. For a long time the liberals in France were ill at ease in the Church because Christian morality declared itself in support of the divine right of kings. In our own day, the most frequent cause of religious difficulties stems from the fact that the current variety of Christian morality makes too strict a connection between the sexual relations of husband and wife and procreation. Fidelity to this morality frequently goes beyond the limits of normal virtue and many, after repeated failure, find no other solution to their anguish than a break with the faith.

Too, the identification of morality and religion harms morality itself. We are all familiar with those who have rejected all religious belief and proclaim themselves atheists. A morality that calls itself Christian and pretends to find its principal justification in a revelation quite logically loses its imperative character for them. But the unbeliever as well as the believer needs a morality founded on precise obligations and these are practically the same for everyone—believer or unbeliever. It follows then that moral obligation is founded on something common to both the believer and the unbeliever.

It is, of course, normal that the believer try to link his moral life with the tenets of his faith. In these he will find the supreme foundation of his morality, the ultimate justification of the generosity it radiates. As Louis Lavelle so well put it in his *Morale et Religion:* "Morality seeks to fortify us and religion to purify us." It is evidently a happy situation when strength goes hand in hand with purity. But our search for the latter ought not serve as an excuse to let our natural human strength lie dormant. To summarize, it is important to distinguish between morality and religion but such a distinction in no way implies a radical separation between the two.

Those who confuse morality and religion, a confusion just as common among believers as unbelievers, are often scandalized when they observe that a fervent practitioner of a religion, who is present at all religious exercises in the parish, is morally inferior to unbelievers. They speak of bigotry and hypocrisy and doubt both the person's religious sincerity and the moral efficacy of his religion. They say: Look at so and so. He never sets foot in church, believes in neither God nor the devil, but what generosity! what honesty! It never occurs to them to conclude that one can be moral without accepting a religious faith and that this latter can be an obstacle to moral development.

As a matter of fact, as we have already noted, the moral level of an individual is more generally proportionate to the degree of his psychic maturity than to his metaphysical convictions. For the comparison to be valid it ought to bear on the behavior of a believer and an unbeliever whose psychic maturity is about the same. In that case I do not think the comparison would be unfavorable to the believer. Generally he draws upon his faith for the motives and necessary energy to rise to a higher level of moral sensitivity.

Sartre and his school, it is true, think that religion is an obstacle to superior morality. "It is because man has been abandoned in a world (without God)," writes Simone de Beauvoir in the *Morality of Ambiguity,* "that his actions are definitive and absolute commitments; he bears the responsibility for a world that is not the work of a foreign power but of himself and in which his defeats as well as his victories are inscribed." We do not wish to argue with this position. There is no doubt that M. Sartre and others have attained a high moral level precisely because they count on no divine support, because in their abandonment they have no other recourse but themselves. But we must note that this is not the case for the majority of those whose lives have no transcendent referent. Far from drawing from their conviction of abandonment and isolation the energy necessary to rise to a higher moral order, they generally become discouraged and renounce even the effort they are capable of. Dostoevsky, who has one of his characters say "If there is no God then there is neither good nor evil and everything is permitted," proves himself to be a better psychologist than Sartre. When St. Paul wrote that if Christ had not risen, that is to say if Christian revelation is not true, then none of man's moral efforts would make any sense, he was evidently not arguing the impossibility for an unbeliever to practice a superior morality. But, like Dostoevsky, he noted the intimate solidarity in the majority of men between moral effort and faith. That this solidarity is weaker today than in St. Paul's time, or for that matter Dostoevsky's time, seems incontestable. Yet it operates in the psyche of many and the fruits it brings forth are far from being all spoiled.

A clear distinction must therefore be made between the identification of a given morality with the Christian religion, on the one hand, and, on the other, the role of stimulus, purification, and elevation that religious faith can afford morality. There is no *one* Christian morality such that the Christian faith depends on it. The latter, on the contrary, must stimulate, purify, and elevate all the moralities which mankind has developed in its long and slow process of maturation. There can be no legitimate objection made if Christian morality endeavors to conserve certain values of the past which men, particularly in times of transition, are tempted to denigrate or underestimate. But it must not become conservative in principle nor attempt to oppose the creation of new values. We believe it is because the Christian moralists of the past centuries were so little concerned with evangelizing the new psychological and social structures that political democracy often tends to anarchy, that the praiseworthy abolition of sexual taboos has given place to promiscuity, and that the movement toward the socialization of property has led to communism and inhuman Statism.

In his conviction of being a collaborator in the creative work of God the mature believer draws a superior moral dynamism from whatever furnishes him with purely immanent motivations. It is not true, contrary to what Marxists and atheistic existentialists believe, that in the Christian perspective the universe is the work of a power foreign to man. Man himself is the artisan of the world, as Teilhard de Chardin has magnificently shown. Knowing that his work is destined to continue beyond this life in no way inhibits the moral will of the believer—quite the contrary.

CHAPTER 11

Emotional Sources and
Motives of Morality

SINCE THE time of Aristotle there have been many attempts to construct a perfectly rational morality. It was believed that if men knew what good and evil were, and where their duty lies, they would act morally. Obviously not every partisan of rational morality thinks that all moral defection is the result of ignorance. Some admit that there can be an evil will, but only because the reason failed to recognize the true good of man as an individual and social being.

We have no intention of discrediting the rational character of moral obligation. Civilized man must try to act rationally or at least be able to justify rationally his moral behavior. The transition from infancy to maturity implies the replacement of a moral obligation that is imposed from without by a moral obligation whose rationality is recognized and which is freely accepted. But however clear our rational knowledge of moral good may be, it is not as a rule sufficient to make us decide to pursue such a good. This is because the pursuit of moral good is generally a very difficult one. The obstacles encountered within us and in our environment are such that our quest of moral good almost always requires a more or less painful effort. Our rational insights are not usually strong enough to motivate our will to action or inspire it to consent to the effort and sacrifices necessary to attain the good.

Further, a purely rational morality would be too inhumanly

strict, too dry, to enable man to obtain his highest fulfillment, to be creative. I have known many people especially before World War I who attempted, under the dominion of the rational prejudices of their age, to live a strictly rational morality. They did good not because they were attracted by it but because their reason imposed it upon them as a duty. An act of charity, for example, done out of pity was in their eyes of lesser moral value. Even relationships between husband and wife, between parents and children were founded on objective duty, excluding all sentimentality. It was the time of *rational marriages* and the fulfillment of *conjugal duties*. Were a woman to seek sensual pleasure in the arms of her husband or give herself out of impulse she would have been severely censured by the current morality.

I once had great admiration for those who lived a rational morality. They submitted to the law because it was the law and not for reasons of pleasure or joy in the fulfillment of their duty. I took such action for heroism. I was later to understand that the first task of morality is not to cultivate *stoical* virtues but to promote individual and collective life, to create happiness. And the psychotherapist knows better than anyone else how rarely happiness comes to those who practice a rational morality.

"Creation," Bergson wrote in *The Two Sources of Religion and Morality*, "is primarily emotion." The moral élan must spring from the love rather than the knowledge of the good. All efficacious morality must be supported by a *mysticism*. The moral progress effected by Christianity is certainly not due to its rational contributions. Other moral systems are incomparably more coherent, rationally more perfect, than that of Christianity. Indeed, the Gospel offers no moral system at all. Its moral teaching can be summed up in these words: *"Love one another as you love yourselves."* Or again: *"Love one another as I have loved you."* By calling forth an unprecedented élan of love Christ enabled humanity to realize the prodigious leap from closed morality to open morality, from conservative morality to creative morality. The contempt of many influential Christians during the past few generations for mysticism, and their pretensions to found their faith on rational evidence alone is certainly not unrelated to the stagnation and growing inefficacy of a morality that still insists on calling itself Christian. The elite of our times, whether in avant-garde of the social or the physical [pure] sciences, have largely abandoned a morality that seems to have lost its creative fire.

It is significant that the promoters of the most clearly defined new rational moralities are confusedly aware, in flagrant contra-diction to their theoretical postulates, that cold reason of itself is not a sufficient basis for a morality worthy of the name. Thus communist morality claims to be materialistic and rational but it makes demands upon its adherents which neither materialism nor rationalism can justify. It is rationally inexplicable that mili-tant communists renounce the comforts of life and sometimes life itself, that they sacrifice their present joys and pleasures to a problematic happy future, that in the hope of the well being, liberty, and happiness of future generations the communist lead-ers believe they have the right to impose upon their people in-finite privations, slavery, and misery; all of this can only be explained on the mystical level. The apparent inferiority of the so-called free world comes largely from its failure to propose a *mystique* to men, demanding that they transcend themselves. Men who have nothing for which they would not be ready to sacrifice their lives are not in a position to create anything truly great.

In our opinion, religious mysticism, because it touches human emotivity most deeply and carries it highest, is better than any other as a source of moral development. But it remains true that a natural love of humanity can serve the same role in the human psyche as mysticism serves in the believer.

In granting emotion, that is to say love and generosity, the primacy in all efficacious and creative morality, we do not intend to profess a sentimental morality that has been and is still so scorned by hardy spirits. Sentiment is the most superficial aspect of affectivity. The moral value of those actions which are inspired by tear-jerking sermons is very slight. One sheds a tear or two and sighs regretfully about the miseries of the world; occasionally one also contributes an extra dollar or two; but it is seldom much more than that.

Moreover, the morality of sentiment is purely subjective; it is content to experience high and generous sentiments without necessarily translating them into positive actions. On the other hand, morality inspired by the deep affectivity of the human heart neither scorns nor underestimates the objective and rational character of moral obligation. Mysticism as it has been understood in the great religious traditions is in no way a vague sensible fervor. It implies lived faith, hope, and charity. It is certainly enthusiastic, but with an enthusiasm that comes from the depth of one's being.

We are not rejecting a morality of duty; it is rather a question of purifying it of too numerous misunderstandings and deformations. It is especially untrue that duty is antipodal to happiness and joy. I would even say that the pursuit of happiness and joy could itself be a duty. Nor is it true that between two conflicting duties we must always choose the most difficult. When there is a choice between love and duty it is generally the choice for love that must be made. To do good to someone one loves in no way diminishes the moral value of the action; quite the contrary, it is always desirable that we love those to whom we do good. Further, we ought to love all of creation and strive to increase its moral content. Nor does sensible joy diminish the moral value of our actions. The Bible teaches that: "God loves him who does good with a joyful heart."

CHAPTER 12

The Maladies of Morality

MAETERLINCK HAS written: "Man is so essentially and necessarily a moral being that when he denies all morality the negation itself is already the kernel of a new morality." Psychologists and moralists are commonly agreed that morality is one of the fundamental functions of man's psyche. We say that certain animals are intelligent; but we never think of them as acting morally.

Unfortunately the functions of the soul, like those of the body, are subject to deformities and maladies. The eyes fail to see, the ears to hear; speech may be impaired and someone who is defined as reasonable and free can be quite unintelligent or the slave of his passions. Some of these maladies, whether physical or psychic, are hereditary and for this reason difficult to cure. Others are due to environment, to diverse accidents that can happen at any moment but principally, in the case of psychic maladies, in infancy and adolescence.

The moral function is also susceptible to deviations and sickness, indeed to premature death. Generally speaking moral health is closely dependent upon general psychic health. Someone who remains at the level of infantile fixations has no chance of achieving a superior moral life and even his ordinary behavior obeys less moral imperatives than taboos and mechanisms.

While many Freudians are inclined to see in morality and its prohibitions the principal cause of neurosis, others on the contrary see it as the most effective therapy of the maladies of the soul. It is true that there are no longer many, even among religious moralists, who consider every psychic maladjustment the result of a moral disorder; but until the nineteenth century it was a widely held opinion. We know today that the sick soul is not the same as a soul in the state of sin or possessed by the devil, and that moral disorder is far from being the unique, or even principal cause of neurosis. Among neurotics are to be found men and women of high standards of morality, indeed authentic saints. On the other hand, there are immoral people whose psychic health is altogether excellent.

Professor Baruk has tried to elaborate a veritable psychiatry of morality. This means psychiatry and psychotherapy postulate certain moral qualities on the part of those who practice them and also that the solution of moral conflicts generally proves to be the *sine qua non* condition of curing neurosis. Our own experience corresponds partially with Professor Baruk's thesis.

Neurosis is almost always the result of a conflict. It may be a question of a conflict between conscious and unconscious psychic tendencies or between tendencies that are all conscious. We grant the Freudian thesis that repression of primitive instincts leads to neurosis; but the repression of moral aspirations often produces an identical effect. Because psychoanalysis so frequently fails to understand the second kind of repression it fails in its battle against neurosis. In our opinion, however, the opposite error, that is to say a misunderstanding of the repression of instincts, would give rise to equally serious failures. It pertains to psychosynthesis to take into account all relevant factors.

The reestablishment of interior moral order cannot be effected therapeutically unless the principal cause of the neurosis was a moral one, namely the repression of moral aspirations. Thus one of my patients could not be cured of his tormenting anguish until he had changed professions for his former profession obliged him to tell frequent lies which repelled his moral conscience. A psychotherapy divorced from all moral considerations would probably have tried to adjust the patient to the necessity of lying in his profession; but I doubt that it would have obtained positive results. It is important to note that when this man came to see me he was not aware of the connection between his anguish and the practice of professional lying. He had already been in analysis and had evidently been advised to seek the cause of his trouble in sexual repressions.

There are certainly cases in which neurosis is the result of the false moral influence of the superego or taboos. Then the task of psychotherapy becomes one of liberating the subject from the tyranny of this false morality. To be positive, however, this liberation ought to lead not to amorality but to a higher morality. It follows that the good psychotherapist cannot be indifferent to moral values. To be sure, his role is not to push the patient toward a moral conversion. In the measure that he becomes progressively liberated from his moral malady he generally orients himself toward a healthy morality. Too, it is important for the therapist to understand that there is a qualitative difference between true and false morality; that the first does not share the neurotic character of the second.

To illustrate the foregoing I have chosen a particularly significant case. Elaine is a young, educated woman. She is not only totally frigid but experiences such a repugnance for the sexual act that she frequently refuses her husband to avoid panic. A painful tension marred the marriage and they seriously considered separation. She had recourse to psychoanalysis as a last resort. It turned out that her frigidity bore a close correlation to a puritanical education which had impressed upon her unconscious the sentiment that sex was impure in its essence. Since purity was the virtue par excellence her unconscious could only experience the sexual act with great guilt. As a little girl she had often heard her mother complaining about her husband's demands, regretting that men needed "such things" which, in her pious perspective, should only be done to have children. As an adult Elaine did not share the maternal condemnation of impure pleasure, but her unconscious remained nonetheless strongly marked by maternal conceptions which she had completely forgotten. After psycho-

analysis had liberated her from the prohibitions of a false unconscious morality she threw herself into the pursuit of erotic
pleasure with a vengeance quite natural after such long privations. Soon her husband no longer satisfied her; she went from
lover to lover, making it a point of honor to attach herself to
none of them.

But two years after her liberation she found herself the prey
of an inexplicable anguish. She was infinitely more unhappy than
before. Once again Elaine addressed herself to a psychoanalyst
who understood her moral personality. In the course of treatment
she discovered that beside, or rather *above* the sexual taboos,
which she had every good reason to cast off, there existed an
authentic sexual morality which could no more tolerate promiscuity than repression. This morality censured her libertine behavior and was the cause of her anguish. To cure this one could
of course have tried to liberate her from the control of this true
morality but what then would have been left of her personality,
herself? She would probably have become like those people who,
under the pretext of being totally free, sow unhappiness and
suffering about them and finally go insane. Psychosynthesis enabled Elaine to regain her sexual health.

In speaking of the moral crisis of our time we noted that many
people are morally atrophied. Their capacity to distinguish between good and evil is not in question and it would therefore be
unfair to establish too close a comparison between them and, say,
those born blind. Their atrophy is incontestably of the emotional order; they feel no impulse to generosity, no attraction
for the good, no aversion to evil. When they commit objectively
immoral acts—such as the wealthy young man who assassinated
an old woman to rob her—they are themselves surprised to find
they experience no remorse. Yet having read in detective stories
that the criminal has a tortured conscience they try to simulate
such grief. Perhaps it is possible for psychotherapy to cure moral
atrophy. But it is undoubtedly true that those who are truly
mutilated morally never consult a psychotherapist. On the other

hand, I have often treated those who were partially atrophied in whom the moral emotional dynamism functioned inadequately, whether as a whole, or at a particular level. After the liquidation of infantile inhibitions all led more significant moral lives.

While psychoanalysis up to the present has never been much interested in the *submorality* of the atrophied, it has from the beginning been very attentive to the *supermorality* that is engendered by unconscious guilt feelings. For numerous psychiatrists all neurosis is the product of the false morality that some identify too lightly with morality as such. What makes morality morbid, that is to say neurotic, says Hesnard, is not submission to a "moral principle," that is to say to a general, collective human discipline resulting from a certain social unanimity. It is rather submission to pre-ethical, infantile values which are in conflict with the natural demands of "the sincere actor man must be in the human drama." With the exception of the apparent identification of neurosis with sick morality, we are in this respect in agreement with Hesnard. Contrary to what he thinks, neurosis, however, is not always and necessarily a conflict on the moral plane although it often is.

Neurotic supermorality does not inspire one to heroic acts, to tend toward a truly superior moral behavior. It gives rise to that painful and very harmful sickness called scrupulosity. This is not to be confused with the normal scrupulosity of sensitive moral consciences. It is extremely important in psychotherapy not to confuse one with the other. While the former has its roots in the unconscious superego the second originates in the adult moral conscience. In practice there is little danger of confusing the two kinds of scrupulosity. The neurotic is tormented by a mere nothing, by the smallest "bad thought," for example, while he is unconcerned about the more fundamental moral values like generosity and charity. There is nothing spontaneous in his hypermorality. His obsession with "purity," for example, does not stem from any superior moral aspiration but is generally founded on an unhealthy fear of sex. The worst sadistic crimes are often the

work of the *too pure*. The altogether imaginary effort to achieve
an inhuman purity gives birth in them to a terrible tension; to
deliver themselves from it they have recourse, half consciously, to
particularly repugnant sexual acts. Normal scrupulosity, on the
other hand, is especially attentive to what is essential in morality.
While the neurotic seeks in himself the measure and criterion of
his perfection, the healthily scrupulous refers to God or the human community, most often to both.

There does exist a *morbid universe of failure* and psychotherapists together with moralists ought to fight against it. But not
every sense of failure is morbid. When I feel guilty of a particular
failure with respect to the human community there can be no
question of liquidating the guilt feeling; on the contrary I must
do whatever I can to make reparation for the fault. True, the
psychotherapist professionally deals most frequently with bad
moral consciences just as the physician professionally treats sick
bodies. Both ought to resist the temptation to conclude from
their clinical experience that all consciences or bodies are sick.
Incontestably the best remedy against moral illness is a healthy
morality. Neither moralists nor psychotherapists ought ever forget that truth.

It is normal to inquire into the causes of moral sickness. In
modern psychotherapy it is well known that the search for the
cause occupies a very important place. In our opinion the mistakes of moral education constitute the principal cause of moral
defection. Too often so much emphasis is put on the purity of
intention that young people scarcely perceive the essential relationship of the moral act with the community of men, with
others.

Moral health and moral perfection are also frequently confused. It is true that the first is generally the condition of realizing
the second. But moral health does not *ipso facto* guarantee moral
perfection. Not every sinner is sick; and just as the best of confessors can do little for the moral sickness we have called scrupulosity, so the best psychotherapist can do nothing for sin. Again,
the saints and wise men who have attained a high degree of moral

perfection are not for all that totally protected from moral sickness. They practice to a heroic degree charity, generosity, justice, and the other moral virtues but because of persistent unconscious motives they can nevertheless be the prey of scruples and feel guilty for nothing. Some of the most admirable saints believed themselves to be rejected by God and trembled in anguish at the anticipation of their own damnation.

Since Freud's time there has been much talk of the harmful effects of repressing the instincts, particularly the sexual instinct. It has even been considered the principal cause of most neuroses. We do not intend to contest this thesis; we have done so at some length in other works. But it is certain that the repression of what might be called the *moral instinct* is just as harmful. So and so discovers that his behavior is in conflict with the moral law. This conflict bothers him but he is not disposed to modify his conduct. He therefore chooses another path which consists in first of all doubting then denying completely the moral law or its foundations. Sometimes this procedure is conscious; most frequently it is unconscious. The subject is then no longer divided between moral obligation and his egoistic tendencies; he declares himself amoral or above the moral law. What actually happens in most cases like this is that the subject merely succeeds in repressing moral obligation. It continues to function in his unconscious exactly as do other repressed instincts, that is to say anarchically. Frequently neurotic troubles develop without any apparent connection with the moral problem. In such cases no analysis can be effective unless, in one way or another, the subject resolves his moral conflict. One must be especially careful not to confuse repressed moral obligation with the infantile taboos which also act upon the unconscious. The distinction between the two sometimes demands great discernment on the part of the psychotherapist. He is obviously not expected to preach morality to his patient; he is responsible for psychic health and therefore for moral health and not moral perfection. The subject himself when he becomes aware of the nature of the problem, will decide what attitude he is going to take. From the point of view of psychic health conscious moral conflict, even if the subject refuses to resolve it by conforming to an interior obligation, is preferable to repression. In religious terms, he who knows he is a sinner is less dangerous than one who, against all evidence, denies the existence of sin.

Another moral malady is melancholy, the sadness following upon the exacerbation of the moral conscience. The subject demands more than necessary from himself and since he cannot fulfill his own demands he becomes discouraged and sadness overwhelms him. Generally he does not know the real cause of his sadness. In any case, he can rarely shake it off without professional help. Hypermorality, or perfectionism, is thus just as dangerous to moral health as the other extreme of refusing to recognize any moral obligation. Those who, in whatever capacity, are responsible for the moral formation of children or adults ought to bear this truth in mind. The task of morality is not to produce heros or saints but men realizing their vocation as men in the community of men. Those who feel called to heroism or sanctity ought to draw the necessary strength from some source other than morality.

Part
~ II ~

CONCRETE APPLICATIONS

CHAPTER 13

Thou Shalt Not Kill

THE MOSAIC commandment prohibiting homicide is common to all moralities. In Hinduism its application extends to everything that lives, including wild beasts and insects harmful to man. Life as such is considered something sacred. The West, more anthropocentric, only recognizes human life as truly sacred and consequently the moral law is intended primarily for man's protection. However, even our morality disapproves of killing lesser forms of life for no reason; it can be justified only in terms of man's protection or nourishment.

Since there is such general agreement on the law against homicide there would be no need to insist on this point were it not for the fact that all moralities, both present and past, admit of accommodations and exceptions in the application of the sacred principle. The principal exception has always been war, so much so that even the disciples of Mahatma Gandhi have resigned themselves to it. To kill a member of one's tribe or nation counts as a crime that is severely punished. To kill as many "enemies" as possible, on the other hand, is an act of virtue and merits high praise from society and most Churches. In the Renaissance, for example, certain Popes personally led their armies to battle, brandishing the cross with one hand and the sword with the other.

It ought to be recalled that in the first three centuries of the Christian era the disciples of Christ were generally inclined to interpret the divine precept in its strictest sense. The universal human fraternity, taught by the Gospel, had effectively succeeded in broadening their awareness to all mankind and they could not therefore understand how a given individual or a given enemy could be considered an "enemy." All this changed when the Church ceased to be a community of believers and became instead the religion of the state. With the end of the Roman Empire and the birth of the feudal society the conscience of the West once more contracted to the narrow dimensions of closed societies. The "Christian" Middle Ages paid only lip service to the sacredness of human life. Its current morality authorized and blessed not only crusades against the "infidels" but also showed itself to be extremely tolerant of wars between Christian princes, murderous duels and, toward the end of the age, approved the terrible Inquisition which burned the heretics. The Middle Ages were succeeded by the era of antagonistic nationalism and revolutionary wars which in turn anticipated massive slaughters of noncombatants by our modern methods of warfare.

However, while the exception became the rule and human life became less and less sacred in the eyes of the lords of war, almost imperceptibly a profound evolution of the human conscience took place also. The multiplication and acceleration of the means of communication, the increase in economic and cultural changes have contributed greatly to a new and very concrete awareness of human unity. Further, the progress of biological and psychological sciences have thrown into relief the grandeur of life in general and of human life in particular. True, we are far from total and general rejection of war by the moral conscience of most men. Politicians can still win applause from crowds by brandishing the threat of war, even a war involving the risk of nuclear destruction. Nevertheless, after World War II, we saw for the first time its principal leaders severely condemned for the crime of genocide and their compatriots themselves approved this judgment. It is interesting too that not a single French bishop ordered public prayers for the victory of the French armies in Algeria, as would have been the case formerly. Most theologians, both Protestant and Catholic, as well as most of the lay moralists were openly against this war. It is not that the Algerian war appeared to them any more unjust or horrible than wars of the past. Rather, the evolution of the collective moral conscience has moved closer to universality. We still reluctantly admit the legitimacy of a war whose defensive character is absolutely evident. But the probable usage of thermonuclear weapons in a new general war makes clear to us the inanity of speaking of legitimacy.

In anathematizing all wars the contemporary moral conscience in no way conflicts with the most traditional teaching of Christian morality. Thomas Aquinas posed these conditions for a legitimate defensive war: that the foreseeable evils be not greater than those being fought against and, secondly, that there be a serious possibility of victory. But today it is more than ever evident that the worst peace is better than the best of war. As for the "possibilities of success," it would be ridiculous to dream of such in a thermonuclear perspective.

Human life is sacred; its destruction whether individual or collective is a crime. In order that this truth become more generally evident and efficacious, moralists ought to follow out the logic of the principles they teach. Religion and morality severely condemn abortion, the destruction of a foetus of a few weeks or months that has not yet attained conscious life, but they are infinitely less severe, if not altogether tolerant, with respect to the supporters of war and capital punishment, even of political crimes. This attitude, in our opinion, reveals an intolerable hypocrisy. We are not favoring abortion. The psychotherapist knows its harmful effects better than anyone. We are simply asking whether or not the interdiction against the destruction of life can allow for morally tolerable exceptions. In any case there is no proportion between the tortures and slaughters of war and the destruction of a simple promise of life in the foetus. The more so since in the latter case we are more often dealing with very painful subjective situations that merit pity, and this scarcely seems the case with warmongers. One common objection to this argument is that abortion kills the innocent while war kills only combatants. This is not the case in modern warfare. Modern wars kill more and more indiscriminately combatants and women, children and old people who are not active participants in the war. Those who admit that war can be morally tolerable in certain circumstances ought to admit that other exceptions might be justified also. In the particular case of abortion, suppose that in certain well-defined cases the decision ought not be left to the individual. The constitutions of almost all states stipulate that the government cannot declare war without the consent of Parliament, which is supposed to represent the voice of the people. Analogous legal precautions ought to be taken with respect to the suspension of any fundamental moral law.

In the name of the sacred character of human life, morality today, in our opinion, ought also condemn capital punishment. To believe that capital punishment checks crime, particularly assassinations, is a serious mistake. It is a well-known fact that crime has not appreciably increased in those countries which have abolished the death sentence. In our opinion what might have some chance of success in checking crime would be the diffusion of the idea that human life is so sacred that it ought to be respected even in the criminal. It goes without saying that we think capital punishment for political crimes against a given regime is particularly immoral. The simple fact that numerous exiles have later become legitimate spokesmen for power and that frequently the people themselves invested them with power dispenses us from developing the argument further.

Suicide is rare in communities where the collective conscience is stronger than the individual conscience. In some vague way individuals in these communities seem to think that they belong more to the tribe or the nation than to themselves. The same is true of those communities in which belief in an after life is strong: why flee the pains and difficulties of this life if one cannot thereby avoid eternal punishment? Only within highly individualized civilizations, such as the Roman civilization in the first centuries of the Christian era and modern civilization for the last century and a half, has suicide been claimed as a right by many and the practice of it scandalizes few. In an individualistic perspective, which always implies a diminution of religious faith, each considers his life as belonging to himself; he seeks only what he believes to be his own happiness and thinks that he has to render account only to himself for the use he makes of his life. Thus nothing could seem more logical than to put an end to one's life when it no long procures the pleasure and happiness desired. Given the quasi-generalization of individualism in the last century it is somewhat surprising that the number of suicides remains nevertheless relatively modest. Albert Camus, who in many ways was the most authentic spokesman for the anguish of men in our time, formulated what he called the most important philosophical problem in a world that no longer believed in eternal life in these words: Why don't men who are convinced of the absurdity of life commit suicide? But neither Camus nor other existentialists of the absurd followed out the logic of their principles. In our opinion this is because a secret voice, scarcely perceptible, murmured in the depths of their unconscious that the individual is perhaps not his own end, that life is less absurd than it might appear and that the notion of happiness is more complicated than individualism would give us to understand.

The perspective within which we are considering certain important moral problems is one of community and person. Thus suicide seems ruled out on the same grounds as homicide. Since human life is sacred and ordered to an end that radically transcends the individual himself as well as every immanent order, no one can dispose of it as he sees fit, whether it be his own life or someone else's. Even honorable suicide (I am thinking here of such customs as that which held that the captain ought to go down with his ship) which was formerly approved does not seem morally justifiable. The only kind of suicide that the moral conscience of educated men today approves is that of a Pierre Brossolette and other resistance fighters under the Nazi occupation of France.

They had recourse to suicide because they were afraid that under torture they would betray their comrades. Such exceptional cases prove that there can be causes more sacred than respect for one's own life, just as there are exceptional circumstances—very exceptional we have seen—that authorize us to administer death to another.

Clearly the risks of death run in the service of a high or moral good cannot be compared to suicide. But again the respect for human life as such demands that the cause for which we expose our lives be of incontestable value. To leap into agitated waters to save the life of another is incontestably an act of moral courage; but the same act done for reasons of bravado or praise from onlookers is not. In order to approve morally the serious risks run by such athletes as mountain climbers it is necessary that they undertake such enterprises with proper training and the right moral motivation.

In the last few decades a specific case of voluntary death has frequently come to the attention of moralists: what must a woman do who is confronted with the painful alternative of not being able to give birth to her child without sacrificing her own life or, on the other hand, of not being able to save her own life without sacrificing that of the child? The sacrifice of a mother for her child is clearly not suicide. But it is an act of heroism and moralists are generally agreed that while heroism may be demanded by mysticism or faith it cannot be imposed by morality. One who covers a friend's body to save him from an assassin's bullet does not commit suicide but not even the strictest morality could impose such an obligation.

The case of legitimate defense, whether of self or others, does not pose a moral problem. Many moralists see here the only case in which it is permitted to kill without moral fault. But it goes without saying that the notion of legitimate defense ought to be understood in a very strict sense. A farmer, for example, has no right to kill someone who is trying to steal his apples any more than we have the right to kill someone who merely insults us.

A certain idea of "honor," toward which the moralities of former times were very lenient with respect to duels, is completely, and let us hope definitively, outdated. Those judges who condemn duelists as assassins express perfectly the attitude of the contemporary moral conscience.

Much more, the contemporary moral conscience is very tolerant toward those who refuse to kill for a legitimate reason. Pacifists, whether or not they be followers of Gandhi, enjoy almost universal sympathy and almost all democratic states give special status to conscientious objectors.

A relatively new moral problem is euthanasia, killing another, with or without his consent, to put an end to his suffering. Our moral conscience obviously disapproves of euthanasia as it was understood by the Nazis who ordered killed all those who were physically unfit or incurable, as well as those considered socially harmful or who simply served no purpose. This notion amounted to a radical negation of the sacred character of human life and elevated the good of a given society to a supreme and unconditional status. It led to the massive slaughter of the Jews and other "inferior races" whose existence presumably cast a shadow upon the "master race." There is no point then in insisting further upon the abuses and horrible crimes that can be committed if we understand euthanasia as a means of ridding society of the unsound, the useless and, finally, the unproductive. There are, however, other cases before which the most demanding moral conscience is puzzled.

In 1961 the court of a large French city acquitted a man who had killed a dearly beloved brother, who suffered from a medically recognized incurable disease. This man, after he had vainly sought the aid of specialists all over the world, killed with a revolver one he loved more than himself; indeed he was willing to be condemned for murder. But the jury noted the special circumstances of the case and acquitted him. Public opinion approved the decision almost unanimously. Only a few Catholic authorities took exception and even they did so with great discretion, thinking more of the precedent thus created than of the particular case in question.

There is no doubt that legal tolerance of euthanasia could give rise to serious abuses and veritable crimes. It is practically inconceivable that a civilized society would leave such a momentous decision to the discretion of individuals. The category of the incurably ill would extend to the point where the sacred character of life would be dangerously compromised. It is well known that there is always a recrudescence of crime, particularly of assassinations, in the years following a war; wartime mentality holds life cheap and the postwar outbreaks are merely a consequence of this. The practice of euthanasia would risk leading us further along this dangerous road.

In principle euthanasia ought therefore remain legally and morally reprehensible. But both law and morality might show tolerance in well-determined, exceptional cases exactly as in other forms of attempts upon human life. The science of medicine, dedicated to the service of life, is quite right to try to prolong life even in those cases where no hope of a cure exists. In acting thus, medicine usually does not do much for the patient in question but it contributes very efficaciously to the maintenance and the promotion of respect for life.

Since the continuity of human life and inferior forms of life can no longer be contested, some of the respect shown the former ought to extend to the latter as well. To wantonly destroy plants or kill animals merits the most energetic moral reprobation without, for all of that, falling into the excesses peculiar to, say, Hinduism. In particular, by teaching children to respect plant and animal life we prepare them to respect human life too and thus to obey the ancient and ever-new commandment of God: Thou shalt not kill.

CHAPTER 14

The Goods of This World

T HE PROGRESS of the moral conscience with respect to property, the possession of the goods of this world, has been quite spectacular in recent times. It is not without importance that this progress has been in the most authentic spirit of Christianity, even though for a long time Christian thinkers and authorities evinced a most reactionary attitude, even going so far as to formally condemn certain evolving ideas about property.

No one denies that man has the right, a right inherent in his nature, to make use of the material goods and all the energies of the earth, and even those that will be discovered eventually on other planets. Human life is not practically conceivable except by the utilization of these treasures whose discovery and transformation has been the principal factor of the progress of the spirit. If we were writing a philosophical work we might be tempted to ask whether or not this right we claim as natural is perhaps too anthropocentric. But such a question is irrelevant to our present purposes. Certain religions, believing in the transmigration of souls, may well prohibit the eating of animal flesh but they do not go so far as to condemn the eating of vegetable forms of life. Modern man does not utilize the resources of the earth in the same way as do animals and savages, who are content to take what nature offers them. Modern man multiplies and transforms the gifts of nature to such an extent that most of the commodities we normally require are much more the result of human activity than a free gift of nature. This fact ought not be forgotten if we are to speak relevantly about the right to property. Neither the moralist nor the sociologist should speak of property in the abstract.

We do not contest the axiom dear to moral theologians according to which the only really *natural* right to property is the right of humanity as a whole to the goods of the earth as a whole. Many concrete and pressing problems cannot be understood or equitably resolved unless we bear that principle in mind. It was on the basis of this principle that Thomas Aquinas, who is rightly considered the principal authority in favor of private property, recognized that the individual had the right to the goods of another if there were no other means of subsistence. But the *first natural right* (the appurtenance of all goods to all men) does not take precedence over the *second natural right* (private property) unless it is a case of strict necessity for the sustenance of life. There is here, however, a hint, in accordance with Teilhard de Chardin's interpretation, of the *humanistic* morality of property. Aquinas' perspective implies the negation on the part of Christian morality of the Roman idea of the right to property—the right to use and abuse those possessions of which one is the master. In the eyes of the Christian moralist who is faithful to the best tradition of his religion, the right to possessions ought to be much more a right—and a duty—of stewardship of goods which really belong to the human collectivity as a whole. It follows from this that a duty corresponds to every right and we are quite correct in thinking that loss of the first *ipso facto* involves the loss of the second.

For several centuries the current morality of the West, which pretended to be Christian, was categorically in favor of private property. Numerous theologians as well as popes have spoken of it during the past century as though it were a sacred right that could not be violated without sin. Serious sociologists and moralists, to say nothing of political leaders, have debated at length whether or not private property could be used for a public high-

way or railroad without the consent of the owner. Thomas
Aquinas is quoted in favor of the legitimacy of private property
and its advantages but those who cite him often omit the restrictions and duties correlative to this right which the Angelic Doctor
himself established. The judiciary annals of the nineteenth century are filled with acquittals for proprietors who manhandled
some luckless chap caught stealing his apples or potatoes.

Fairness, however, obliges us to note that if Christian morality
tended more and more to conceive of private property as absolutely and sacredly as did Roman law, it was owing in large part
to historical circumstances. In the Middle Ages the popes and
bishops were often at odds with fringe sects who generally denied
the legitimacy of private property and attempted to do away with
it by violence. Further, the Church, because of the confusion
between the temporal and the spiritual that prevailed in that
age, was the principal property holder, and to defend private
property was tantamount to defending herself against the heretics as the Body of Christ. The recent pontifical documents which
take such a strong stand in favor of private property can be explained as reactions against the socialists and communists, who
heap the same scorn upon Christianity as upon capitalism. It is
evidently very regrettable that, with the exception of a few isolated Christian thinkers, the most authorized defenders of the
faith let themselves be trapped into ratifying the confusion of
Proudhon and Marx between religion and a particular social
regime.

As a matter of fact private property is in its essence neither
more nor less "natural" nor more nor less "sacred" than collective
or communal property. It is well known, and let it be well noted,
that primitive communities which are closer to nature than we are
are ignorant of private property. The earth and the waters belong
to the community as a whole. As the goods furnished by brute
nature began to be developed and increased artificially, private,
or rather family property became a reality. The latter however is
no less natural than tribal property, for as we pointed out in the

first part of this book, as man evolves his creative activities do not
become in any way unnatural; quite the contrary, it is in thus
evolving that he actualizes his potentialities.

As for the sanctity of private property, it should be pointed
out that no mention was made of it in the Christian tradition
until the eighteenth century. The first to talk about it were the
English economists who were trying to legitimize and justify a
nascent capitalist regime that was menaced by the anger of exploited people. Throughout the first Christian centuries the most
celebrated Fathers and Doctors of the Church looked upon private property as a second best arrangement, a consequence of
egoism and the stain of sin; some of them went so far as to attribute its origin to Satan. In an unequivocal manner all of these
Doctors favored communal property.

"In the primitive state of humanity," writes Gregory of Nyssa,
"mine and yours, those baleful words, were never used. . . . As
the sun and air are common to all, and as above all God's grace
and blessing is common to all, so too were all other goods held
in common and the perverse desire to get rich was unknown."
Since this was the original state of things decreed by God, the holy
Bishop concluded that Christians ought to strive to reestablish
that state. Ambrose, Bishop of Milan, thought in like terms. He
wrote: "The Lord willed that this earth be the common possession of all men and that its fruits be for all." And John Chrysos-
tom, Bishop of Constantinople, said:

God has given us the sun, the stars, the heavens, the elements, the
rivers. We enjoy them in common; none of them is appropriated. No
expenditures or legal processes regulate their distribution. This is the
image of the law of nature. It is very certain that the reason for which
God placed all of these things at our common use is his will to teach us
by such examples to likewise possess all other things in common. It is
because some wish to monopolize what belongs to all that quarrels and
wars break out, as though nature were indignant that man, by means of
the cold expression "mine and yours," puts division where God has
put unity. . . . The community of goods is a more adequate form of
existence for human nature than private property.

We have referred here to three of the most venerated representatives of the Christian tradition, both in the Eastern and
Western Church. It would be easy to multiply quotations since
on this point the tradition is practically unanimous. Thomas
Aquinas in the thirteenth century seems to have been the first
of the great doctors to declare himself decidedly on the side of
private property. We have already noted some of the limitations
and obligations with which he qualified this right. But it is significant that Basil, Ambrose, and other Fathers were speaking in
terms of a Christian ideal of life while Aquinas was merely trying
to argue circumstantially. The goods of the earth, Aquinas
argued, are limited; if they are to satisfy the vital needs of all, a
rational administration of them is imperative. But experience
proves that man is more concerned with what belongs to him
that with what belongs to all. If each is responsible for the
administration of a determined and limited quantity of goods
then they will be handled in a more orderly fashion and the
confusion and conflict that stem from an indistinct possession of
all goods by all men will be avoided. If each contents himself
with what he has then human relations will be more peaceful
than in a regime of collective property. (*Summa Theologica*, IIa
IIae, q. 66)

We do not propose to contest the grounds of Aquinas' argument for it has been supported by a number of pontifical documents, especially Leo XIII's social encyclical *Rerum Novarum*.
As arguments of convenience and circumstance they are of incontestable worth for a given historical and psychological state
of the human condition. But since this condition is modified in
terms of human development we in no wise show disrespect for
Aquinas's doctrine in asking what form of property best corresponds to the present situation of mankind. It is further important to note that since the Christian Church is not only the
community of those who aspire to evangelical perfection but has
become a social institution, it practices two moralities with respect
to property. The Church estimates that private property is more
adapted to most people; but of those who vow themselves to

perfection she does and has always demanded a community of goods.

We are not interested here in eternal essences. Thus it is not our intention to argue that one form of property is better in itself than another. The noumenal order is inaccessible to the psychological and sociological sciences, sciences upon whose evidence we are trying to found a new morality adapted to the dynamic and dialectical situation of modern man. The analyses of Aquinas and Marx are of equal justice since both probably express well the situation of their respective ages. Still less do we wish to point out the divergences between the positions of Leo XIII and John XXIII. Such divergence can be explained, even in the particularly narrow perspective of the Vatican, in terms of the differences that exist between the historical reality of man in 1961 and man in 1881.

Not only have men changed but the term "property" is far from indicating the same reality today as it did only a century ago. Until the end of the nineteenth century the debate between the partisans and adversaries of private property was directed principally to goods for consumption such as land and money. St. Thomas More and those after him whom we call social utopians recommended that all goods be held in common; in this they followed the general inspiration of the first Christian communities in which, according to the Acts of the Apostles, all was held in common. Work in the fields and in the shops was done cooperatively, the members of the community lived in a kind of barracks, ate the same food, dressed alike and so forth. The extremists of utopianism went further: there was to be no individual sexual partner and children were to know no other parents than the community. It is easy to understand how such doctrines so disturbed popes, bishops, and all others who were attached to permanent moral and human values.

Today the problem of property cannot be discussed at the same level. There is scarcely an economist or a sociologist who would advise the abolition of that private property which Christian moralists rightly considered the extension of the person and the family. Private property is a reality even in communist countries. Those who can afford it own an automobile, and sometimes a home, indeed even a country home. There is no question, at least in the foreseeable future, of abolishing monogamous marriage or remitting the care of children to a collectivity. To my knowledge the only ones who are still at least partially faithful to the ideal of a communist utopia are those small groups of fervent Christians, especially in France, who have founded agricultural or industrial communities in which the common life is practiced. But their inspiration is neither Fourier nor Saint-Simon but the example of the Christian communities of apostolic times.

The problem of property today centers primarily on the means of production and the sources of energy. If the small business has difficulty maintaining itself it is due less to the enemies of private property than to the general evolution of modern economy and the laws of concurrence. Big corporations as a result tend to become more and more gigantic and can scarcely be compared to family enterprises of earlier times. In a family business the employer was both proprietor and owner. In such a circumstance it was relatively easy to specify the proprietor's rights and duties; they were much like those of a proprietor of a small piece of land, a factory, or a small sum of money. Quite different are the large-scale business concerns of today whose financial and technical directors are not the proprietors; generally speaking the proprietors do not take a direct hand in the running of the business. Ownership is, in effect, divided among a number of shareholders who are only interested in making money. Nothing is more instructive in this respect than a general meeting of the shareholders in a large firm. As a rule they do not discuss matters of production or social questions; they speak only of dividends and the allotment of profits. It could scarcely be otherwise when the same company owns a bank in Paris and another in London, rubber plantations in Vietnam, oil wells in the Sahara, and so forth.

The problem then is this: is it morally admissible that the

stockholders alone control the profits of a business or eventually decide to close it down if it does not pay as much as another business? We cannot forget that the workers (and we use the term in its most extensive sense to include the middle and managerial classes) contribute by their labor as much as does capital to the life of the company. Further, their lot and that of their families is much more bound up with the company than that of the capitalists. Moreover, the real control of modern business does not rest so much with the capitalists as it does with the financiers and technocrats who act in their name, being at least theoretically mandated by them. There is this further fact: the immense sums of money at the disposal of big business confers upon its directors a power that is susceptible of going beyond the economic level and threatening in a dangerous way the indispensable autonomy of political power. The machinations of "warmongers" are not merely legendary.

It thus seems evident that the morality of property in the traditional sense no longer corresponds to the new reality. Some states, including France, hoped to remedy the situation by nationalizing the sources of energy, the railroads, banks, insurance companies, and other branches of the economy that are closely allied with the general welfare of the nation. Other countries, particularly Germany where the memory of a state with excessive powers is still very much alive, hesitate to have recourse to this solution of the problem of property. It is interesting to note that in France, Italy, and even America the most fervent partisans of nationalization and other limitations of private property are to be found among Christians; this is not the case in Germany; quite the contrary, the politically committed Christians hesitate the longest before taking action on necessary changes. Probably the fact that one-third of their country is under communist domination explains at least in part this state of affairs; it is quite natural that they fear anything that remotely resembles communism.

It is evident that nationalization as it is understood today does not imply the abolition of private property as it was traditionally understood. An equitable indemnization of property is imperative in the name of morality; but this in no way prevents private capital from profitable deployment in nationalized enterprises. Since profit is at least theoretically the fruit of labor, we see nothing immoral in remuneration for services rendered. In this perspective those who control the capital are no more the proprietors of the business than those who comprise the labor force.

We are not in favor of a tentacular state which, like Russia, would be the only proprietor of the country's wealth. The dangers implicit in this kind of control are at least as great as those we denounce in capitalism. The term that seems most appropriate to express a regime of property best suited to our age is *socialization.* Teilhard de Chardin used this expression whenever he discussed social problems. Pope John XXIII in his encyclical *Mater et Magistra,* in reaffirming the legitimacy of private property (and let us recall that what is legitimate is not always obligatory), also recognized the legitimacy and the necessity of complementing this right with socialization. Evidently he understood by socialization something more than the classical "social duties" of private property.

Nationalization understood as *statism* is a category of closed morality. Thus the Soviet economy, completely subjected to the politics of the communist State, long unscrupulously exploited even other communist countries. It took the revolutions in East Germany, Poland, and Hungary in 1955–56 to force the Kremlin to revise its economic policies with respect to the colonies. But even today Russia and China display their economic power as imperialistically as the capitalist nations. Thus they render economic assistance to those governments that serve their political interests and withhold it from those who do not.

Socialization, as we understand it, is by contrast a category of open morality. It admits that in certain well-defined cases the state may be the proprietor of the enterprise and even manage it directly. This is particularly necessary for those activities that are exclusively in the interest of national defense. In other cases, socialization may mean nationalization in the sense that France and other countries have nationalized electricity and gas, railways and certain branches of heavy industry. The enterprises retain their character of a moral person and operate as much with private and public capital while the state exercises a function of control and guardianship. However, it is desirable that a greater share in the management and general responsibilities of the enterprise be granted to qualified representatives of the personnel. The promotion of humanity, which every worthy morality ought to promote, requires that the workers acquire a consciousness of being not simply *employees* but *members* of the enterprise. Business would then take on more explicitly the character of a community.

Given the supranational structure of much economic and political activity, socialization of property cannot be limited to nations. At least some particularly important forms of productive activity ought to become *internationalized*. The example of the European Six seems to be a first step on the path to transcending national boundaries. Already there is a problem of international, or supranational, property with regard to the production of thermonuclear energy and very likely analogous necessities will emerge on other levels.

Cooperatives and communities of work represent still another form of the socialization of property. Even agricultural communities which, at least in France, are usually associated with the traditional meaning of private property, are undergoing a profound transformation. The agitation on the part of young farmers in the past few years indicates such a transformation. They consider the land not as the symbol of wealth but as the instrument of their labor. Unlike their parents and grandparents, for whom the acquisition of a plot of land represented something very precious, they have centered their activity primarily on the revindication of the rights of those who work the land. They do not hesitate to call into question the sacrosanct rights of property when a proprietor uses his land in a way that is contrary to the interests of those who live off the land. It is interesting to observe that the communists did not inspire these young agricultural movements; their leaders were almost all formed in Catholic action movements and remain Christian.

But the difference between the partisans of socialization and the communists is still enormous. The former do not hold that private property is immoral by nature. As long as private property fulfills its social responsibility and promotes the common good there can be no question of attacking it. When the common good calls for some form of socialization or other those who hold private property ought not be exploited but equitably remunerated. The partisans of socialization do not share Proudhon's celebrated slogan: "Property is theft." And, as we pointed out earlier, there is no reason why private capital cannot be profitably invested in socialized enterprises. It is only the monopoly of capital that is coming more and more to be considered immoral. Moreover, in the communist regime, at least as it exists in many countries, socialization is a mere juridical fiction. In fact all of their productive goods belong to the totalitarian state which disposes of them as arbitrarily and with as little regard for general interests as private capitalism.

The new morality still has much to do before property fully accomplishes its task in the service of humanity. Agricultural cooperatives, for example, certainly represent considerable moral progress by comparison with the ferocious individualism of former times; but if they become a closed concern, without respect for the interests of other social categories, they cannot claim superior morality. Supposing that socialization of property were perfect within a given nation; now if this were to become an instrument of domination and enslavement of other peoples morality could not approve of it. We must never forget the fundamental truth that anteriorly to all divisions and allocations the goods of the earth belong to all mankind and, above all, humanity is one and indivisible. It is incontestably immoral for a state to order farmers to destroy a crop in order to maintain a balance of prices while other people are hungry. We cannot but regret the relative silence of religious and moral authorities before such abuses of property which are still unfortunately too frequent. We cannot but salute the decision of the European economic community to create a fund enabling it to place the surplus of production of rich countries at the disposition of poor countries, provided of course this is effected without any intention to dominate.

In recommending as universal as possible socialization of property we are not in any way falling prey to the old utopian temptation for general egalitarianism. However seductive such an ideal may appear in theory, its realization is not possible in terms of the present development of humanity. Today that ideal is a reality only in small communities like monasteries whose members are animated by a supernatural motive and have deliberately renounced the right to possess the goods of this earth. And this is more an egality of dispossession than an egality of possession. Even in Russia, the model country of communism, no one dares hope for total equality after the disastrous attempts of earlier days in this direction. It is taken for granted that the political and economic leaders have their villas on the Black Sea, their limousines, and their expensive shopping centers while the average Soviet citizen cannot expect the same advantages.

However developed be our idea of human unity and the social function of property, we cannot morally condemn a certain hierarchy in the use we make of the goods in our possession. It is quite legitimate that the producer, individual or collective, look to his own needs and those of his dependents first. Even if all the children about are starving a mother is quite within her rights to give the only piece of bread she has to her own child. By the same token the basic needs of our distant brothers ought to take precedence over our own desire for nonessentials and luxuries. But under no circumstances can we morally justify the destruction of goods for consumption as long as abundance is not the lot of all the inhabitants of the earth.

Closely connected with the right of property is the right of inheritance. If we agree that it is not immoral to possess goods or the means necessary to their production then we cannot object to their transmission by heritage. If it is moral for us to turn our labor to profit during our lifetime then there can be no objection to willing what we have acquired to our descendents. Haven't we all profited by the material and spiritual legacies of generations and civilizations that have preceded us? Human progress would be impossible if each generation were obliged to start with nothing. This is also true in more restricted domains such as the family. An awareness of the universal solidarity of man ought not lead us to forget or neglect more limited solidarities and particularly family solidarity. A particular right ought to be open to the universal but not be absorbed by it.

The moralist's principal difficulty in justifying inheritance stems from the capitalistic possession of the means of production, whether they be industrial or agricultural. It is morally intolerable that an individual become by inheritance the proprietor of a factory in which he does not work or of lands that he does not till for by virtue of this inheritance he acquires exorbitant rights over the fate of a number of workers and their families. But if it is understood that the property of the enterprise is no longer the prerogative of capital then there is no objection in principal to the transmission of this latter to heirs. If, on the other hand, an excessive concentration of capital harms the common good then the state has every right to intervene. This has effectively been the case for a long time since most countries impose heavy taxes upon inheritances.

CHAPTER 15

By the Sweat of Thy Brow

O F ALL human activities work is invested with an especially high moral value in our day. But it has not always been so. Not only in relatively uncivilized societies but even in the ultrarefined Greco-Roman civilization work, which was unworthy of a free man, fell to the slaves. Historically, work became a moral value as a result of the Christian influence. Christ did not belong to a superior caste; he was a village workman. He recruited his apostles from among fishermen and laborers; Paul, for example, exercised the difficult trade of tent-maker.

It was probably with the birth of monasticism in the beginning of the fourth century that the ascetic character of work began to receive emphasis. For Christ, as for Paul, it was a means of livelihood as, especially for Paul, a means of independence and disinterest. But the hermits in the desert had few needs and could well have lived a life of leisure. But it was precisely to avoid the spiritual and moral dangers to which leisure gives birth that the masters of monastic life imposed on themselves and their disciples a strict obligation to work. Thus they imitated the command of God, as recorded in the book of Genesis: "Thou shalt earn thy bread by the sweat of thy brow." It ought to be recalled that in the same biblical tradition God had charged man to fructify and increase by his labor the created order; that is to say, work was considered a positive benefit before it was made a punishment for sin. But even as a means of purification and penance work took on a superior meaning for the Christian while the pagan world saw in it nothing but a humiliating and degrading form of servitude. Even the serfs of the Middle Ages, however painful their condition may otherwise have been, were aware that their labor in spite of all had human and supernatural meaning. Despite whatever criticism may be directed against the illusion of celestial rewards, it cannot be denied that such rewards played an important psychological role in the lives of men who were overwhelmed by the yoke of labor and who did not have the means to lighten their burden.

Moralists began to consider the problem of work in a fresh light only very recently, actually since the industrial revolution so fundamentally modified the traditional modes of production. This modification went hand in hand with the increasing secularization of social life in suchwise that many men could not be satisfied with the secularized Christian conception of work as a means of penance and redemption. Marx, in particular, noted that in the nascent capitalist society work was only one commodity among others; it could be bought and sold in conformity to the law of supply and demand. Socialism was to put an end to this alienation and restore to man the fruits of his labor. There is no doubt that Marx contributed immensely to the dignity of the laborer and to an awareness of the nobility of his social function. Of course, from the point of view of economics not all goods that are useful to man are the product of manual labor. Today especially many other agencies contribute to the production of wealth. But it was psychologically good that the worker become aware of his nobility and social importance even though at times he tended to overestimate it. Work was no longer a curse; on the contrary it bestowed upon man his supreme dignity in making him the benefactor of humanity.

Perhaps the greatest contribution of Marxism in this respect is to have stimulated Christian writers to rethink the problem of work in fresh terms. The perspective of a materialist philosophy is in effect insufficient to give work an authentic moral value. Economic activity is certainly necessary and worthy of man; but man cannot be reduced to a *homo economicus*. The purpose of morality, as we have said, is to enable man to accede to a superior degree of humanity, to promote man as a spiritual character. Work must effect this to be a moral value. But an economic perspective alone is too limited to favor such a promotion of man. The concomitant reflection of philosophers, theologians, naturalists, and workers themselves have come to the conclusion that the work of man creates much more than the economic goods necessary to his subsistence and that of his brothers; it is by his work that man becomes man.

No philosopher so elevated work as did Bergson. The author of *The Two Sources of Morality and Religion* held that it is by his work that man becomes a cocreator with God. Creation is in effect a continuous divine act; it is continued in the immanent process of the evolution and maturation of the universe, but in a more intelligent and more conscious manner by human work. Work produces value, not only in the economic sense of the term, but it helps create being, the very stuff of the universe. Teilhard de Chardin went even further along these lines, if that were possible. He wrote.

In my work I am united to the creative power of God. I am identified with him not only as an instrument but as his living continuation . . . Everything with which I enrich myself and things adds to my capacity to love. . . . Whether we be artists, workers, scholars or engaged in some other human activity, we can dedicate ourselves to our work as a means of fulfilling our existence. In the totality of our activity God reveals the depth of his being.

When the early Christian moralists spoke of work they were thinking especially, if not exclusively, of manual labor. Marx also thought it was principally the laborers who would constitute the proletariat which in his mind was to renew the face of the world. In making ours the sublime ideas of Bergson and Teilhard with respect to work, we are also thinking of the laborer, the factory worker, and the miner; but we do not exclude the engineer, the manager, the professor, the writer, the scientific researcher, or any other intellectual. Indeed, in our opinion the spirit is necessarily engaged in all human work; and the more it is engaged the more human is the work. It is in no way contrary to what we may consider "the natural law of work" that man, thanks to technical progress, has succeeded in making machines do the larger part of physical labor. The highly qualified technician who operates a complicated electronic machine is no less a true worker than the manual laborer who breaks rocks with a primitive hammer. In fact he is much more so because in his work the specifically human faculties are more effectively mobilized. We cannot then but salute technical progress that tends toward an increasing "humanization" of work. It would be absurd to think that it contradicts some divine commandment.

Let us note parenthetically that the struggle of workers against nonworkers no longer makes any sense. And communist propaganda presents its case less and less in these terms. Instead of the "rights of workers" it now speaks more of the "rights of the salaried." But this has no precise meaning since almost all members of the upper levels of society today are also salaried. The proletariat as Marx knew him toward the middle of the nineteenth century no longer exists in economically advanced countries. The social effort today must be concerned with a more equitable distribution of profits among the different categories of workers. The present situation, in communist as well as capitalist countries, in which the earnings of the worker are emphasized to the detriment of the managerial classes is not fair.

Again, we are not arguing the case for egalitarianism. Even from a strictly economic point of view it is not true that all workers contribute quantitatively and qualitatively in the same degree to the production of wealth. In principle, each ought to be remunerated according to his work. And while it is possible to measure the quantitative contribution of each participant it is practically impossible to measure his qualitative contribution. Thus remunerative justice can only be approximate, a condition that in no wise dispenses us from the task of rendering it as perfect as possible.

From a moral point of view, all forms of work are not of equal value. Few forms of work are downright immoral. But morality is not simply the opposite of immorality. Again let us stress the point that moral activity ought to create something positive; it ought to be a creative activity. There is thus a moral hierarchy between different kinds of work according to whether or not the worker converts it to more or less positive values.

We cannot approve the attitude which has prevailed among many Christians of considering all forms of work of equal value; to be sure, one endowed with limited ability can reach a high degree of moral perfection by dedicating himself to humble activities. But the same is not true of those with superior gifts who, either out of laziness or from a badly understood humility, refuse to use them. This is clear from the most authentic Christian doctrine. We have only to recall the parable of the talents. The Lord was very angry indeed with the servant who, instead of multiplying the one talent that had been confided to him, buried it for reasons of security. The master's anger with him who had been given five talents would have been just as great had he failed to multiply them, or if he had only multiplied one of them. The progress of civilization, as well as the growth of the individual in the order of the spirit, are conceivable only on condition that we maximize our talents and our capacities.

We take the first criterion of establishing a moral hierarchy of work to be its social influence. The man who works only for the satisfaction of his own needs may be very moral subjectively; but his work is morally inferior to someone whose work is of more universal magnitude. Thus because of the implied universality of modern enterprises we can say that the work of contemporary man is objectively more moral than that of the man of yesteryear who only worked for his family or his village. But for an act to be authentically moral the objective and subjective elements ought to coincide as perfectly as possible. There is a certain kind of objectivity that it just as morally objectionable as subjectivity. Ideally, then, our work ought objectively serve the most universal human good and, subjectively, we ought to have the intention of working for the good of humanity. By making our moral intention coincide with the objective moral value of our work we can realize important advances in the morality of work.

thy brow" points to a consequence of sin. But Christ has, by His work of Redemption, conquered the reign of sin. The Christian who places higher moral value on work that is painful or boring is effectively denying the efficacy of redemption. It is true, as St. Paul reminds us, that redemption is an historical project rather than an accomplished fact. But it is not by resigning ourselves to the negative aspects of work that we will contribute to the completion of Christ's redemptive work. It seems to me that any social or technical progress that diminishes the pain of work and increases its joy implies a victory over the reign of sin. As Teilhard de Chardin said so well, the believing Christian ought to find greater happiness in his work, and give himself to it more enthusiastically, than the unbeliever. For, unlike the latter, the believer is conscious of working not only for the perfection of a perishable terrestrial city but also for the construction of the eternal city of God.

CHAPTER 16

Nationalism and Love of Country

A PREFERENCE FOR the country of one's birth is probably as old as man himself. There is something like osmosis between the individual and his environment. This environment is evidently conditioned in the first place by the physical reality of the climate, the vegetation, and the animal life which determine the eating and clothing habits of the individual. But language, customs, religion, and culture are equally integral parts and therefore enter into a definition of the country.

Love of country is generally considered one of the fundamental moral virtues, as the natural extension of the love one spontaneously feels for one's parents. Moreover, society, however primitive or evolved it be, has every interest in that its members experience the liveliest patriotic sentiments possible, for its cohesion and strength are partially dependent upon them. Almost unconsciously, by a simple vital reflex, it does everything to maintain and increase patriotism. Almost until the advent of Christianity each country had its own gods and worshiped them in a manner that excluded strangers. Christianity itself has always had great difficulty in affirming its doctrinal universality practically. Especially in time of war the faithful, together with bishops and priests, are only too inclined to make of the Christian God an exclusive God of their people and count on him to make their armies victorious. A German Catholic magazine recently took a kind of malicious pleasure in printing a series of episcopal statements, made during the two World Wars, which all testified to the identification of the Christian God with the Germanic god. But such a confusion is far from the sole privilege of German Catholics.

We are almost universally convinced that it is not enough to submit to the laws of our country but further that we must be ready to sacrifice our lives in its defense and glory. Whence the necessity of conferring upon the country a sacred, indeed specifically religious, character. Socrates preferred to obey the laws of his country, however unjustly they were administered in his case, rather than flee. The cities of every country erect monuments to those who died in war. I knew a German priest who was solidly opposed to the Nazi regime and never missed an opporunity to denounce publicly Hitler's crimes against humanity. But on armistice day in 1945 I heard him preach a highly emotional sermon on the sublime sacrifices the German soldiers made for their country, as though they were martyrs of the faith! It was hard to convince the good priest that the Gestapo torturers and other leaders would also have to be counted among his patriotic heroes. In his mind the soldiers were obeying the momentary laws of their country and were thus innocent of the crimes committed by the Nazi leaders. The latter alone were responsible. Such abuses of the obligation to love one's country imply grave dangers and oblige us to reexamine the moral justification of patriotism.

In fact the idea of the fatherland is not more eternal and immutable than the other concepts that clarify our intellectual and emotional lives. In the course of the long development of human history, it has also undergone transformations proportionate to the evolution of conscience. When, for example, Socrates' compatriots began to refer to themselves as Greeks rather than Athenians an important breach was made in the walls of closed society.

Since the French Revolution there has been a close synonymy between country and nation and, consequently, between patri-

otism and nationalism. In spite of the proclamations of universalist faith on the part of the orators of the Revolution, nationalism
was from the beginning a return to closed society. The civilization
of medieval Christianity was in fact cosmopolitan. An Italian
could be prime minister to the King of France. A Frenchman
could be a bishop in Germany. The wars were not so much between peoples as between princes. For neither the mercenaries of
the emperor, nor those of Francis I, nor those of the King of
Spain, nor those of the Duke of Milan were conscious of fighting
for their country. They liked the adventurous life of war and
offered their services to those princes who paid most. Thus, for
example, some of the citizens of Milan were for the Sforzas and
others for the King of France; but neither group was considered
traitorous. The love for Lombardy was probably equally intense
in all. During the Renaissance poets and scholars sang the praises
of Italy in spite of the political dissensions and antagonisms that
divided the country.

Nationalist patriotism is directly opposed to other nationalisms.
Often to preach the love of country is at the same time to preach
hatred of other countries. Modern wars are thus no longer the
affair of princes; nationalist propaganda presents them as the
sacred cause of the peoples themselves. As good patriots the French
hate the English and, of course, the Germans as "hereditary
enemies." Long before Dr. Goebbels elevated lies and calumny
to the rank of patriotic distinction nationalist propaganda practiced both *ad majorem patriae gloriam.* For the French patriot
the German was the *boche,* heavy-spirited, incapable of imagination and initiative, happy only when he could carry out orders
and march in rhythmed step. For the German patriot, the Frenchman was the *welsch,* superficial and vain, perfumed but un-
washed, while French women were all empty-headed and loose of
morals. Similar clichés are part of the patriotic complex of every
people with regard to their neighbors.

Traditionally nationalist patriotism has been identified with
the conservative right while the left professed an international-

ism, indeed the most radical cosmopolitanism. Enlightened spirits were accustomed to proclaiming the whole universe their country; they regarded themselves as citizens of the world and made fun of the narrow-minded patriotism of the bourgeois. In Germany they invented the expression *hurra-patriotismus* which was clearly not intended to flatter.

But politicians observed, despite the mockery of the intellectuals, that nationalist and patriotic sentiment was very much alive among their peoples. Hitler and his cohorts exalted it to the point of paroxysm and succeeded finally in leading a highly cultured people into the folly of war. Stalin, feeling his power over the Russian people threatened, abandoned the old internationalism of socialism and appealed to the patriotic nationalism (or nationalist patriotism) of the Russian people in order to mobilize their energies against the threatening danger. The French communists followed the Russian lead in this respect and declared themselves ardent "patriots." Both during and after World War II they have endeavored to exploit the patriotism of peoples in the service of their own cause. They have appropriated the terminology and slogans of the extreme right nationalism of former times. It is now the communists who are reviving the ancient myth of an hereditary enemy to block the formation of a West European community, something they judge to be dangerous to the interests of the Soviet state. The worst insult the communist press can hurl at their political adversaries is to call them "cosmopolitans." It is an old but ever-new story.

We do not believe the communists are sincere in the question of patriotism and nationalism. They play on these sentiments as a tactical maneuver of propaganda. And while it has been effective in Russia, the communists are certainly not going in the "direction of history" by making themselves the paragons of nationalism. Such narrowness is from all evidence a definitely outdated phase of the evolution of the collective conscience.

The harm done by nationalism in the recent history of the West is such that the moral conscience of a psychically mature man can only condemn it. The fact that nationalist propaganda of extreme rightists finds little echo with people today is a significant sign of moral progress. This is true of France and Germany as well as the other Western countries. Even England is breaking away from her insular tradition. We may be mistaken but it seems hardly possible that any form of nationalist propaganda could ever again lead the French and Germans into war against one another. If there be wars to come they will be waged in the name of myths other than the myth of the nation. It is only in excolonial and underdeveloped countries that the nationalist complex retains its explosive dynamism. It is undoubtedly one of the worst legacies they received from their former European masters and we can only hope that this crisis of growth will be shorter than in Europe and that it will result in less damage.

Because of the identification between nationalism and patriotism during the last two centuries the discredit that has fallen upon the former will in all probability affect the second as well. Not that patriotism no longer plays a role in the collective conscience of peoples. In exceptional circumstances, as for example the occupation of a country by a foreign army, it can become very strong. But upon closer examination we must acknowledge that there is a great difference, for example, between French patriotism in 1914 and that of World War II. It was truly for the defense and glory of the country that the soldiers and people waxed enthusiastic in 1914 in crying "To Berlin." The patriotic emotion that is evidenced in the official documents and the journalistic writings of the time as well as in the letters of soldiers and civilians has an authentic ring about it. The same was true of other countries at war. Only a few intellectuals like Jaurès and Romain Rolland in France and Liebknecht and Rosa Luxembourg in Germany together with a handful of anarchists wanted to "be above the masses." Generally both the right and the left in all countries shared a common patriotic faith.

The case was quite different in World War II. The call to arms in 1939 was not met with national unanimity. In the first place, because Russia was the ally of Nazi Germany communist propaganda was deliberately defeatist. After the fall of France and the German invasion a whole segment of French citizens, traditionally the most nationalist and patriotic, rallied enthusiastically to the conqueror with whom they felt ideologically more at home than with their democratic compatriots. The latter, for their part, in their efforts to organize the Resistance were thinking far more of the democratic liberties to be reestablished than of the triumph of a humiliated country over the hereditary enemy. The communists became "patriotic" resisters when Nazi Germany became the enemy of the Soviet Union and thus threatened the communist regime. These are all events that can scarcely be squared with the traditional notion of patriotism.

Another example of the growth of the moral conscience with respect to patriotism is furnished by recent history in France. President De Gaulle, carrying on the tradition of nationalism and patriotism in good nineteenth century style, set himself against the formation of a supranational Europe by putting forth his idea of a "Europe of countries." But despite the personal prestige of De Gaulle with the French people his thesis fell upon deaf ears. I have discussed this subject with a number of Frenchmen of divergent social and political backgrounds. I have not met one who thinks that the continued existence of France within the inevitable and desirable unity of Europe is worth fighting for or, for that matter, even getting excited about. Even those who are politically committed to advancing De Gaulle's platform do so with little conviction. I have noticed a similar dilution of patriotic sentiment in several other European countries.

No good psychologist would want to see the energies formerly called forth by patriotism totally atrophied. In a fully human life no energy ought to be left untapped. Moreover, emotional forces that are not used are repressed in the unconscious and are likely to emerge later in explosive and cataclysmic forms. Nationalist patriotism, a characteristic of closed society, is certainly outdated both by reason of changes in the objective situation and in the conscience of mankind. But the energies formerly absorbed by nationalism must be orientated toward other goals; otherwise demagogues like Hitler could still breathe warm ashes into a flame of chauvinism and thus mercilessly impede the cause of human unity. The new morality must promote a new patriotism, one freed from the mire of nationalism and fashioned to modern man's universalist awareness.

But can there be an *open* patriotism in the Bergsonian sense of the term? That is to say, a love of country that does not feed on hatred of other countries? With few exceptions men of the past were not capable of this and indeed there are many today who have not reached this level of awareness. The latter have ceased to be partiots in the nationalist sense of the word without having made any emotional commitment to a vaster community. They are for Europe or for the West for reasons that are strictly pragmatic; but their hearts are not involved.

In some quarters the solidarity of classes has become an emotional substitute for nationalist patriotism. This substitution commenced with the workers over a century ago when Marx, in *The Communist Manifesto,* set forth his famous appeal: "Workers of the world, unite!" With a simplicity that is surprising in a man of such genuine historical culture, Marx taught that national frontiers were artificial boundaries erected by the capitalists, that there was no country for the proletariats, that the only bonds of human solidarity they ought to recognize were those of class solidarity. Of course there is no doubt that the mystique of the class played an appreciable role in ameliorating the material condition of workers. It further contributed in some degree to enlarging the perspectives of human awareness. Other classes—bourgeois, peasants, professionals—have endeavored to imitate this example; but they cannot claim the same success as the proletariat.

It is our opinion that the substitution of a class mystique for a nationalist-patriotic mystique is not a mark of real moral progress. The class is as closed a reality as nationalism; it can only affirm itself in opposition to other classes. Indeed, Marx spoke of class struggle as the motor force of all human history. Some of his disciples went so far as to declare *sacred* the hatred which the proletariat ought to manifest toward other classes. But as we have noted in the first part of this work love and not hatred is alone capable of promoting human existence to a higher level of authenticity. Even in the Marxist ideology a future classless society is anticipated in which class struggle and hatred would be logically excluded.

There is nothing in what I have said to encourage pessimism. There are already large numbers who experience authentic patriotic sentiments for "our mother the Earth" as a totality. Many men and women of all countries consider themselves infinitely more members of humanity than of a nation, a class, or a race. These men and women especially are in the forefront of the arts and sciences. Because of their creative influence it is not rash to hope that more and more converts will be won to the cause of a *universal country*.

Universal patriotism does not exclude any reasonable attachment to the corner of the earth where we were born, or where we spent our childhood, or where we spent a good part of our life. There often exists a kind of preestablished harmony between a given person and a given country or countryside. A universality that did not take into account certain particularities would risk being purely abstract and therefore inefficacious. To pretend to love humanity without loving those people who are closest to us is a dangerous illusion. Likewise it is in loving Provence, Britain, Bavaria, Scotland, or Sicily that we learn to love the universe. The love of a small section of a country is much more likely to avoid the pitfalls of a closed affection than national patriotism. Provence has no army, no desire for economic domination, indeed it has no precise boundaries. Just as one can be a good Provençal and a good Frenchman so one can be a good Provençal and a good European, indeed a perfect citizen of the world. Such small-scale love can best avoid hateful rivalries if universal patriotism is solidly rooted in the depths of our psyche. If it is true that the universal is real only as a synthesis of particulars, it is equally true that the particular realities are truly authentic only as integral parts of the universal.

What we have just said is equally valid for families, races, classes, and even religions. Universality does not imply uniformity. Partial forgetfulness of this truth during the feudal ages seems to us the principal cause of the spiritual and moral calamity that disunited Christians. Since the Church acted more Roman than Catholic she could not help excluding from her fold those who psychologically, geographically, or culturally could not be Romans.

One of my friends, a reputed biologist, calls himself a "racist." Teilhard de Chardin also spoke of the immense differences he observed between different races. But both the Jesuit and my friend are sufficiently aware of human unity; their "racism" does not imply any contempt for other races. I might well observe that a given race is biologically and psychologically different from the French without for all of that considering them inferior. As a reaction to the racism of yesterday, notably the extreme form of racism represented by Nazism, our universal awareness often remains abstract. In the name of human equality we propose, and often impose, political institutions, moral codes, and systems of thought upon the Africans and Asians which are in no way adapted to the specific structures of the respective races and which, because of this, can only prove to be inefficacious, if not altogether harmful to moral progress.

Although I take my Catholic faith seriously, I see nothing scandalous in that others seek God by other ways. This strikes me not only as normal but desirable. Would the Catholic Church be making such praiseworthy efforts to de-Romanize and universalize her administrative structures and her modes of thinking if numerous Christians were not separated from her? Personally, my spiritual contacts with Islamism and Hinduism have helped me enormously in understanding the profound implications of my Christian faith. I am not suggesting an amalgamation of all religions under some vague common denominator; it is by remaining themselves that they will be able to enrich one another mutually and contribute to the spiritual progress of humanity.

It is difficult to say whether the Marxist hope of a classless society will be realized. In any event the Soviet Union is far from projecting an image of such a society. In my youth I labored many years for the advent of a classless society; today I wonder whether or not it is desirable. What seems more important is that societies not become closed castes, that countries not become closed nationalisms. Classes, races, churches and countries ought to be as open as possible; class consciousness as well as patriotism ought to be integrated into the larger awareness of human unity.

CHAPTER 17

International Relations

Formerly the principal chapter in books on international morality treated of war and peace treaties. Moralists tried to *humanize* that essentially inhuman reality which is war. At bottom, although this was not stated explicitly, moral problems were posed and solved within the framework of a closed community, the national state; international morality was merely an additional chapter. Today it is impossible to speak of international morality as though it were a different kind of morality. As we have said repeatedly in these pages the moral conscience of the evolved man of the twentieth century does not recognize racial or national frontiers. The material and spiritual relationships between peoples have become so complex that the ministers of foreign affairs are well on their way to becoming anachronistic; almost all ministers must concern themselves with international questions and are in direct contact with their counterparts in other countries. It follows that most of the moral problems we have treated or will treat must be formulated in international terms.

The questions we wish to take up in the present chapter concern relations between states and peoples. The most important of these questions is the peaceful *coexistence* between states whose ideologies and economico-political systems are radically opposed. Materially, the problem is by no means a new one. In the Western Europe of the last few centuries we witnessed first antagonism between the Protestant and Catholic countries, each trying to exterminate the other. Then the Republic that issued from the French Revolution believed itself called to rid all nations of their "tyrants" while the latter, in the name of the divine right of kings, looked upon the annihilation of the republic as a sacred duty. Little by little, however, the liberal principles of tolerance became more generalized to the point where scarcely anyone contests the right to co-exist of such diverse forms of government as monarchies, absolute or constitutional, republics, and even dictatorships of the Latin American variety.

Communism declared to the world its intention to conquer but no one took it seriously. Stalin sent as representative to the League of Nations the highly sophisticated Litvinov, a man well-schooled in the ways of diplomacy. It was expected that the Soviet regime would die a rapid death, whether natural or violent; meanwhile relations with Russia posed no special difficulties. This was particularly true since Stalin seemed to have no intention of carrying the revolution beyond his own country, occupied as he was with fighting his internal enemies and trying to establish "socialism" in Russia. That country was thus treated along the lines of classical diplomacy as one state among many.

The situation has totally changed since the end of World War II. Partially as a result of their original mistake in treating Russia as one state among others, the Western powers have permitted her to extend her dominion over Eastern and Central Europe. On the other hand, communism has been victorious in an important part of Asia. Thus Russia has become a major military and economic power, and this partially with the help capitalist allies gave her in the war against Hitler. Stalin, haunted by the bitter memory of the German invasion, began to worry principally about the consolidation of his empire; he was concerned to make it as invulnerable as possible. His successor, Khrushchev, is more ambitious and more optimistic. He has entered his country squarely into worldwide competition and extended its influence to the excolonial countries of Asia and Africa as well as Latin America, which the United States has always considered its private preserve. The new Russian leader frequently reminds the world that the political drama today is not unfolding in the traditional style between the great powers but between diametrically opposed ideologies of which one, obviously his own, is infallibly destined to triumph. Not content to develop the old theoretical argument of Marxism to the effect that the final triumph of communism is dialectically necessary, he bases his arguments on the facts most likely to impress the world: Russia's supremacy in the conquest of space and thermonuclear weapons.

It is altogether natural that peoples who hold different values be mortally afraid of Russia, to say nothing of Red China. They do not believe that Khrushchev's proclaimed desire for peace is sincere, especially in view of the fact that he has made it clear he intends to take advantage of the peace to insure the worldwide triumph of communism by means of what he calls *peaceful competition*. How can nations defend themselves against this threat?

There are still military and political leaders who regret that the United States did not take advantage of their thermonuclear superiority of some ten years ago to annihilate Russia with a "preventive" war. Others think that in the present state of equilibrium between the powers the so-called free world ought to risk war to put an end to communist expansion.

Need we point out that morality cannot in any way approve this kind of solution to the problems raised by communism? First of all the chances of a preventive war being successful are minimal for the success of communism in many poor countries seems far from being entirely due to communist propaganda or the military power of Russia. But above all, as we indicated in Chapter 13, the thermonuclear war with which we are threatened is so radically immoral that no cause, however legitimate or sacred it be, could justify it. Who with even a minimal moral sense would dare justify the horrible atomic slaughter of Hiroshima and Nagasaki? How, then, can one even contemplate the destruction of all life, perhaps for centuries in entire countries, that would be necessarily the result of a war with the new weapons?

War is an easy solution to the contradictions which confront international relations at this time; and like all easy solutions it is a false solution. However unsatisfactory the present peaceful coexistence between communism and the democracies seems to be, it is nevertheless the only moral solution. It is obviously regrettable that the antagonists cannot trust one another and sign a meaningful peace treaty. But history reveals that peace treaties do not prevent wars. Peace among peoples as among individuals can only be a dynamic reality on the condition that it is continually willed anew. To pretend to establish it once and for all by immutable treaties can only give rise to dangerous illusions. The awareness of insecurity that has been our lot since World War II can itself be a motivating force for peace since it forbids us to rest upon any false or precarious sense of security.

Peaceful coexistence, even in a competitive sense as Khrushchev wants it, would naturally be much more acceptable to peoples if it were not constantly threatened with the possibility of warfare. From a moral point of view we cannot but approve all efforts toward general disarmament, and especially toward banning thermonuclear arms. But unfortunately we must take politicians for what they are. This means that if we consent to peaceful coexistence only after total or partial disarmament has taken place, we risk losing whatever slim chances remain for man's survival. We are well aware of the terrible fragility of a peace founded solely on the balance of power but morality, to be efficacious, must take the facts as they are however little they resemble the ideal.

Loyal acceptance of the principle of coexistence among peoples, which in present circumstances is a moral necessity, could contribute very effectively to moral progress in general. The war instinct in nations is much like aggressiveness in individuals. Both are rooted in unconscious insecurity feelings, even though they may be overcompensated by superiority feelings. In a climate of relaxation confidence in self and in others may be born and grow strong. In this case feelings of inferiority and insecurity will become less pronounced; then aggressiveness in individuals and the instinct to war in nations are susceptible of decreasing and even of disappearing altogether. The result would be greater tolerance, a liberalism in the best sense of the word. Then co-existence would be peaceful not only in its exterior form but also in its essence. This hope is not entirely chimerical; for at present conflicts between diverse political and economic systems show signs of diminishing. While the soviet regime is becoming more tolerant toward private initiative and even solicits it, the liberal democracies are getting away from traditional "capitalism." This evolution in international relations on both sides gives us some ground to expect a new climate, different from that of the cold war.

A new problem of international morality is raised by the formation of huge economico-political blocs, of which the European Six is a notable case. Poorer countries observe with apprehension the union of economic powers among some of the richer nations.

Thus as we have said before the moral progress of humanity is tending toward the transcendence of dispersions and divisions, toward the realization of a more and more complete unity. Humanity will be truly adult when its conscience is truly universal. The overcoming of feudal disunity by the formation of nations represented a step forward, despite our criticisms of nationalism. European unification is incontestably in line with the same historical movement of maturation. It would be desirable if the whole European continent could form a single economic and political community. This for various reasons is not yet possible; but the steps that are being taken in this direction are highly justified. Furthermore, since the West-European community seems to have succeeded in reconciling Germany and France, whose rivalries in the past provoked the worst of catastrophes, the cause of international morality is still further advanced.

The apprehensions of the poorer nations would be well founded if the European community became a closed society, standing in opposition to other countries and trying to dominate them. The peace between Germany and France would be a small benefit indeed if it gave place to a new rivalry, for example, be-

tween Western Europe and the United States, or the Soviet bloc
or the poorer nations. There is no doubt that such a danger exists.
Many politicians are still too imbued with the spirit of nationalism not to want to inject this spirit into a higher community
which by design wishes to be supranational. The European community should close its doors to no country on the continent that
would like to join it and should consider itself as of now a fore-
shadowing of a worldwide community. Meanwhile it ought to
share some of its wealth with the poorer nations for it is only at
this price that world peace can be guaranteed.

It used to be the case that treatises on international morality
gave a large place to the delicate problems raised by colonialism.
Since this problem, at least as it has existed since the nineteenth
century, has almost disappeared it might be thought that there is
no reason to speak of it here. In fact only one form of colonialism
disappeared with the independence of almost all the countries
colonized by the great European powers. But the relations between these new states and economically and culturally prosperous countries raise problems which are quite different from those
which concern relations between nations whose maturity is
roughly the same.

Certain words take on a more mythical than realistic meaning,
having become like the symbols of good and evil. There is a
reluctance to examine their objective content. This is the case
with the words "colonization" and "independence." A moralist
who would attempt to contest the value of one and defend the
value of the other would inevitably pass for a reactionary; he
would be suspected of complicity with imperialism and colonialism. Yet we must recognize that the independence of most of the
countries of Africa, Asia, and even Latin America is extremely
fragile; it is far more evident in the halls of the United Nations
than in the daily lives of the peoples concerned. Their low cultural level makes it practically impossible for them to avoid
falling under the more or less discreet tutelage of one or another
of the great powers, to avoid becoming satellites of one or another

of the blocs that are engaged in the cold war. Frenquently their only independence consists in the power to choose more or less freely their tutor, to give their allegiance to the party that offers the most.

Colonization in itself is far from being immoral. Until World War II the most liberal of moralists had no difficulty justifying it. They generally made use of the same principles that traditionally served to solve moral problems concerning property. When a people, they reasoned, was not capable of advancing its own civilization or exploiting its own resources then it ought to be directed by a more evolved nation, exactly as a mine-owner, for example, who is not capable of administering his mine ought to let a more profitable concern do it. The tutor in such cases must exercise his direction primarily for the good of his pupil but he could legitimately claim remuneration for services rendered. In this perspective the only immoral form of colonial power would be one which disrespected the primary rights of the native population or held power after the colonized people became capable of managing their own affairs.

This morality was not entirely false; nor can we rightly say that its partisans were hypocrites. Colonialism was a fact and moralists had the duty to make moral judgments about it. Nevertheless this *colonial morality* was up against practically insurmountable difficulties. First of all, who was to decide whether or not a people was sufficiently evolved to manage their own affairs? The moralists answered: an international society. But such a society did not exist at that time. After World War I, for example, Germany's excolonies were divided among the victors simply because they had won the war. In fact the domination of colonial peoples was effected by the use of force and moralists could only try a posteriori to induce respect for the rights of native peoples and urge the colonizers to educate and civilize a people they had conquered.

We are scarcely in a more advantageous position today with the problems of neocolonialism. The United Nations does not give Russia its rights of domination over central European countries and the Balkans, nor the United States its privileged position in Latin America, nor France and Britain theirs in Africa. The agreements of "mutual" aid and cooperation signed by the great powers with the rulers of the underdeveloped countries (or, euphemistically, countries "in the process of development") are most frequently mere fiction. The same is true of the agreements signed between Russia and the communist rulers of Poland, Czechoslovakia, and so forth. These leaders abrogate in a highly arbitrary manner the right of their people to speak—either because the people lack sufficient education for a true democracy or because, as is the case with the Soviet satellites, they look upon their leaders as having been imposed upon them by a tutelary power. It follows that we, too, find ourselves before a situation of fact which we must attempt to justify morally as much as possible.

The exploitation of one people by another is just as immoral as the exploitation of one man by another. To oblige, as is presently the case, underdeveloped countries to sell their products cheaply while they have to pay dearly for the manufactured products that are offered in exchange is unquestionably immoral. And just as immoral is the kind of bootlicking that certain leaders of underdeveloped countries enthusiastically engage in vis-à-vis the stronger powers.

But, under pretext of fully respecting the independence of the underdeveloped countries, it would also be immoral to abandon them to a miserable autarchy. In the name of human solidarity the rich nations have a serious obligation to render assistance to the poor nations, and civilized nations to help those which are as yet not. The prosperity of a country is not measured in terms of its global wealth, which may well be in the hands of a few individuals, but by the equitable distribution of the general wealth among all. Likewise we cannot consider humanity evolved and prosperous because a small number of nations have reached a high degree of culture and material prosperity while the majority of nations are deprived of the indispensable minimum of material and cultural goods.

Prosperous peoples in coming to the aid of poor nations ought not do so in the spirit of almsgiving; they are merely acquitting themselves of an elementary moral obligation. But in order to prevent such aid from becoming a means of domination and, consequently, to prevent it from giving rise either to rivalries among the great powers or extortion on the part of the smaller countries it necessarily ought to be administered by truly supranational agencies. It would have been a considerable moral step forward had, for example, aid to the young African states which had formerly been French, English, or Belgian, been administered directly by the European community rather than by the former colonizers themselves. Presently rivalries exist, and others will likely develop between the excolonies and Russia and even the United States, just as there are rivalries between Russia and China in the matter of foreign aid. Thus the equitable distribution of wealth and other forms of assistance ought to be organized on a global scale.

While the contemporary moral conscience disapproves of colonialism as it existed for the last century, implying the enslavement of weaker peoples by stronger, as well as of neocolonialism, it would nonetheless do well to take a stand on another form of "colonialization." We are speaking of a colonialization as it was understood by the Greeks and Phoenicians who, overpopulated in their own countries, founded more spacious "colonies." Overpopulation is a serious problem in many parts of the world today, especially in Asia where it is fundamentally impossible to feed all inhabitants. On the other hand there exist in Africa, and especially in America, vast unpopulated regions. It is not morally permissible for the governments of such countries jealously to close their frontiers. Whatever national interests exist, massive transfers of populations have become an urgent necessity, both from the political and economic points of view. It is greatly to be hoped that mankind will soon become adult enough to realize this indispensable form of "colonization" in a peaceful manner. Otherwise, we seem certain to court invasions as was the case with migratory peoples in the past. Again, if this kind of colonialization is to be effected peacefully on the gigantic scale that is necessary today, a truly worldwide authority must be established.

CHAPTER 18

The Best Form of Government

Among the many forms of government that exist in the world today can we say that one or another of them is morally superior? Some twenty years ago I taught a course in sociology and psychology at a Catholic institution of higher learning. The program given me by the administration indicated, among other things, that the evolution of political systems favored democracy. The reference was obviously to parliamentary democracy as it existed under the French Third Republic. Such teaching represented remarkable courage under the Vichy regime and the Nazi occupation. And, although somewhat simplistic, it was also an act of faith in human evolution. This is all the more remarkable in that the immense majority of French Catholics had long adhered to the theory of the divine right of kings and were resolutely opposed to democratic republicanism. Too, the *Action Française* movement of Charles Maurras campaigned violently in favor of monarchy, a monarchy that was heavily compromised by fascist tendencies. The adherents of this movement believed that royalty alone was the best form of government, for all countries and all peoples.

The Marxists, on the other hand, believe that supreme happiness for mankind will be the result of a classless society; the dictatorship of the proletariat under the communist party's guidance is in their mind the most moral form of government. In Lenin's words: "What favors the advent of communism is moral; what opposes it is immoral." Once communism is solidly established

everywhere there will be neither state nor government thus realizing the ancient anarchist dream of a humanity so generous and
so perfect that it will spontaneously promote the common good
free of any authority.

The quarrels over the best form of government among both
political theoreticians and practitioners is usually based on a static
conception of morality. Thus the United States, which is justly
proud of the success of liberal democracy which has enabled them
to create a highly structured nation with extremely heterogeneous
ethnic and religious elements, is too inclined to make an article
of faith out of democracy. The Americans are almost as convinced
of the divine right of democracy as formerly people were convinced of the divine right of kings. With a relentlessness that no
failure can stem they endeavor to make liberal democracy prevail
among the newly created nations. The United States pours great
sums of money into the said nations for fear that without such aid
they will drift away from the democratic ideal. They do not understand and are scandalized that the great North American democracy has not been emulated in Latin America where one coup
follows another, one dictatorship is succeeded by another. And
they are genuinely shocked that the new states of Africa and Asia
have not succeeded in establishing a democratic form of government despite massive financial aid. They blame a malicious communist bogey man who outdoes them in aid and thus attracts
political leaders toward a more or less openly dictatorial form of
government with a unique party whose chief does not draw his
power from universal suffrage but rather from the party, unless
of course he himself has created the party and continues to direct
it and symbolize its spirit.

In reality there is no political regime that has divine sanction;
no regime that is alone legitimate or the best for all peoples at
each stage of their evolution. Political morality like the morality
of property must take into consideration that humanity is certainly one, but that this is a unity in an infinite diversity. Human
nature, we have said, is less something given than a task to be

accomplished. Depending upon circumstances, very divergent political regimes are in keeping with natural and indeed divine law provided they respond to the exigencies of the common good and promote human evolution.

In our time parliamentary democracy seems effectively adapted to the psychological and sociological conditions of the Anglo-Saxon and Scandinavian peoples and those who more or less resemble them. It doesn't matter much whether or not these nations call themselves republics or constitutional monarchies because in either case their power comes from universal suffrage and is exercised under the control of parliament. Is the success of democracy in these countries the result of their material prosperity? There is probably a reciprocal influence. All of them are Nordic; even within the amalgam of North America itself the Nordic element is preponderant and for a long time almost exclusively held the reins of power. These peoples are as a rule not very passionate, more pragmatic than "mystical," and, perhaps precisely because of this fact, rather easily disciplined. With few exceptions, small minorities whose sympathies are with dictatorships of either the right or the left, the majority of the inhabitants of these countries adhere rationally and emotionally to a democratic form of government. Of course the laws of social evolution also obtain in these countries. Thus Sweden, although a country that is very attached to parliamentary democracy, has lately tended more toward socialism. Great Britain, after World War II began in a similar direction but later reversed itself. Even the United States, where sentimental attachment to liberal democracy is most pronounced, evidences a certain evolution towards socialization.

Is the German peoples' strong natural penchant for mysticism, with what that implies of periodic and sudden eruptions of irrationality, what has until now made them so inept at democratic government? In addition, they are naturally disposed to obedience which they readily identify with love of order. After World War I the Weimar Republic modeled its institutions as much as possible after those of the French Third Republic; but these were so ill suited to the spirit and soul of the German Republic that only a small minority adhered to them sincerely. We know today the lamentable failure of this first attempt at democracy in Germany. The Nazis did not have much trouble taking over a power that was practically nonexistent anyway. If the Nazis had not done so the communists most certainly would have.

The second German democracy which has been in power since World War II was fashioned more along American than French lines. Is it for all of that more stable, more "natural" to the German soul? I do not doubt the sincerity of a great number of Germans, whether politicians or simple citizens, in adopting a democratic government. The Nazi experience was a shattering one for them and their sincerity in forming the kind of government that seems to account for the power and prosperity of the United States and Nordic countries cannot be questioned. But the spontaneous political reactions of those Germans I have talked with seem far from those of the Americans, the Swiss, or the Scandinavians. They take pains, to be sure, to avoid anything that smacks of mysticism and irrationality. But they are still generally inclined to confuse order with unconditional submission to established authority. The political parties they have formed, with clearly defined ideological structures ("*weltanschaulich*"), bear little relationship to the pragmatism of Scandinavian and Anglo-Saxon parties. Further, the Germans continue instinctively to worship the *strong man;* consequently one man can hold power for a long period of time and there is a danger that at some future time one of these strong men, even though he may have come to power as a result of democratic procedures, will become a new dictator.

We are convinced, however, that even for Germany, in the present historical age, the best form of government is a democracy. But the German people themselves must be responsible for their democratic education. They ought to elaborate a distinctively German form of democracy and renounce the vain imitation of French or Anglo-Saxon democracies.

Among Latin peoples only the French have any lengthy democratic experience. Latin peoples, unlike their Nordic brethren, are frequently excessively individualistic which favors the periodic explosion of their inclinations to anarchy. In conformity with the usual process of overcompensation they alternate anarchy with dictatoriships of the Mussolini, Franco, or Salazar variety—dictatorships which are significantly different from those of Hitler and Stalin. Since 1945 the young Italian democracy has closely imitated French democracy, with all of its virtues and all of its defects.

The French people are unquestionably attached to democracy. Yet parliamentarianism has never functioned in France as successfully as in Scandinavia or in the Anglo-Saxon countries. The multitude of parties, the lack of civic sense, and a natural distaste for collective discipline has catapulted the French government from one crisis to another. The crisis we are presently undergoing may well spell the end of the parliamentary system. But we should not identify this with democracy as such and therefore conclude that the end of democracy is imminent. French democracy is in search of new structures; it seems that the peasant and worker syndicates and the various economic, professional, family, and cultural organizations will be called upon to play in the new democracy a role analagous to that which the political parties so ineptly acquitted themselves of in the old. The close collaboration already begun between some of the large syndicates and organizations of young farmers, teachers, students, and so forth, gives grounds for hope that the new cells of French democracy will be less closed that those that have prevailed until now. If this is so then the present changes augur well for real moral progress.

The democratic form of government seems viable and effective only in economically and culturally evolved countries whose population for the most part can participate—evidently to a greater or less extent—in public life. It would therefore be a mistake to wish to apply the same system, in the name of a static and abstract political morality, to nations that have not attained the same degree of maturity. We cannot morally approve the communist dictatorship of communist countries. Yet a pseudodemocratic regime could never have accomplished in Russia what communism did. The easy comparison between India, theoretically a democracy, and communist China is very instructive in this respect.

Concerning the underdeveloped countries of Africa and Asia and the majority of the countries of Latin America, where a minority are capable of understanding public affairs, the moralist does not have to opt for either democracy or totalitarianism but has rather to choose between a personal power exercised by men with an interest in the common good and a power concentrated in the hands of a few greedy men. The powerful democracies of the West cannot possibly prevent the underdeveloped countries from going communist simply by providing financial and military support to corrupt politicians who call themselves partisans of democratic liberties. True democracy can take root only after a long evolution and even then it ought to be wary of imitating Western democracies. We also believe that the communist regime is undergoing progressive democratization; here again the democracy that may eventually emerge will be quite different from that of Anglo-Saxon parliamentary democracy.

CHAPTER 19

The Family,
a Fundamental Moral Unity

THE SOCIOLOGISTS and social reformers of the nineteenth century, inspired by a simple-minded view of evolution, were very wrong in predicting the more or less rapid disappearance of the family. In the perspective of a rampant individualism the family seemed to be the chief obstacle to the total emancipation of the individual. Even the Marxists, at least after Engels, considered the family as it has traditionally existed to be one of the dispensable structures of capitalism. Thus to fight against the capitalists was to fight against the family. In the future communist society the individual was to be directly integrated with the state, insofar as there would be any state. Stable marriages would disappear and children, born of occasional relations, would be educated in state-run institutions.

It is well known that the communists tried to put this theory into practice in the first years of their regime. The tragic results of the experiment are equally well known. Free love became libertinage. A veritable epidemic of suicides followed among women who had been abandoned and deceived after brief encounters. The children who were raised by the state were unstable and unhappy; many of them joined the ranks of the famous *bezprizorni*, vagabonds and criminals who seriously threatened the public security of Russia. The authorities had to admit the complete failure of their antifamily policy. With customary abrupt-

ness Stalin adopted a diametrically opposite policy. Free love
was once again disapproved of by official morality, divorces were
harder to get than in most capitalist countries and parents were
again charged with the education of their children. Some communist theoreticians, trying to save face, argued that the reversal
of policy was a temporary tactic made necessary by the lack of
communist maturity on the part of Russian citizens and that one
day there would be a return to the original Marxist-Lenin theory
of the family. Today no one in Russia speaks of the abolition of
the family, although leaders are nonetheless quite as hopeful of
the realization of the perfect communist state. Moreover, Khrushchev travels all over the world in the company of his wife and
children, a spectacle that formerly would have been considered a
typical manifestation of "hypocritical bourgeois sentimentalism."

Thus from an ideological point of view the family seems less
threatened today than it did some thirty or forty years ago. The
celebrated line of a great writer: "Families, I hate you!" that so
scandalized or aroused the enthusiasm of men and women of a
generation ago seems today an incongruity in very bad taste.
Nevertheless, behind the façade of renewed prestige, the family
is undergoing a profound moral crisis. Family problems are quite
as serious as those of society.

By its nature family unity is closer, more rooted in the biopsychic structures of human beings than in any other society or
group of people. This unity is gravely compromised by the present tendency of young people to look upon the home as a kind
of hotel where one sleeps and eats. At the root of this attitude are
the modern exigencies of work. The place of work, or the school
in the case of the children, is usually located far from the home;
one leaves early in the morning to return only in the evening.
Members of the family are usually too tired to do much in common except eat and even this isn't always possible since they
sometimes return home at different times. All familial communication is thus abolished; it is not surprising that young people,
and even parents, prefer to spend their free time and holidays
with friends rather than with each other.

If the family were like other groups there would be no reason to regret its dissolution in favor of wider circles of association in which members feel more at ease than in the family itself. But, as we have said, the family is not an ordinary society; it is certainly not an ephemeral one. It is, as the title of this chapter indicates, the *fundamental moral unity*. Within the family one serves his apprenticeship in solidarity and responsibility. Any psychologist knows the instability and insecurity of those who have not benefited by deep family roots. Thus we can only approve the efforts of parents to restore the "rights of the family" and make them respected by even the adult children.

But it would be wrong to try to restore the old patriarchical conception of the family. This would correspond neither to the sociological nor psychological realities of our time. Thus, for example, it is no longer possible to consider children or servants as *things* belonging to the family without the right to personal tastes and relationships. Today children can have friends at school or at work whom the parents do not know; mixing of different social classes is also quite in order. To some extent this is also true of the parents. Formerly it was inconceivable, especially in middle class circles, for parents to have friends that weren't common to both parties. The wife would be bored in the company of her husband's friends and vice versa. They went out together or they stayed home. Compromises are always necessary in family life. But it ought never be forgotten that however strong be the bonds that unite family members mutually they are still individuals endowed with autonomy. By properly encouraging this individuality the family itself will profit.

Too, the family is more restricted today; and this seems to be irreversible. In other times uncles and aunts, cousins and grandparents were part of the family. This was a psychological counterpart to the old patriarchical family which no longer exists as a sociological reality. Today relatives are not normally considered as belonging to the family. Even married children move out. While there is a desire on the part of adult children to remain on good terms with other members of the family, they have a distinct awareness of founding an autonomous family when they marry. One consequence of this is that there is no longer the same need to please in-laws. The adage, "One marries a man or a woman and not the parents," is in perfect keeping with the modern mentality and the most demanding morality cannot change it. Indeed, many factors that formerly made conjugal harmony difficult are for this reason eliminated, although it must be added that good relations on all sides is something to be desired.

We can understand the nostalgia of older people who remember the days when even the servants were considered at least theoretically part of the family. They often spent a lifetime in the service of the same masters; they weren't paid much but on the other hand they weren't dismissed when they became sick or old. Mores have changed. No one wants to be a servant today; some more euphemistic title is used. Domestics want to be paid according to union wages and protected by social laws. Domestics today no more consider themselves part of the family than the factory worker considers himself part of his boss' family. The morality of work rather than family morality regulates relations between families and their domestic employees. The only thing that pertains to family morality is to see to it that the children treat the servants not as objects belonging to the family but as human persons who have in no way lost their dignity as a result of their work.

Nor is it as evident that the father is the uncontested and incontestable head of the family. Today the woman, whether she has a profession or not, wants to be considered the equal of her husband in everything that concerns the running of the household. In some families, especially among the working class, the wife seems to have become the head. The husband hands his paycheck over to her and she is totally responsible for managing the home. Likewise the education of the children is considered the domain of mothers; the father at most being called in for occasional advice.

It would be ideal if family authority and responsibility were exercised mutually by both husband and wife. Moreover, most young homes have abandoned the vestiges of the patriarchate without having fallen into a matriarchate. It is desirable, too, and quite in keeping with the democratic spirit of our times, that the children become progressively associated with the exercise of responsibility in the family. It follows that the children ought to share family expenses as soon as they begin their professional careers. The custom, in middle-class families as well as among the working class, of letting children who work keep their earnings as pocket money can hardly promote adult responsibility. We have observed numerous cases of the disorder that many young people encounter in marriage when they have not been sufficiently trained in the school of responsibility. Criminal tendencies are also fostered by this failure. It is our opinion that an allowance proportionate to the resources of each is preferable to a fixed allowance. One advantage of this is that those members of the family who are not yet wage earners won't feel so much like parasites.

Much more explicitly than for political society, which is founded primarily on justice, or for the diverse economic and cultural societies based on common interests, love is the cement of family unity. Conjugal love is the cornerstone of this unity; upon it is built parental, maternal, filial, and fraternal love. Such love in no way excludes authority, which we will discuss later, nor mutual respect, nor justice. Traditionally there was much emphasis on the childrens' obligation to respect their parents but less on the parents' obligation toward their children. Further, children must respect one another. All of this implies and demands discipline—a discipline, not administered with inflexibility or formalism but with simplicity as becomes those who love one another.

The greatest danger families currently risk is of becoming closed societies. In the beginning of this century, frightened by the transformation of traditional values, many Christian families, especially among the middle class, believed they could protect themselves from the hostile world only by turning in on themselves. Children had to attend schools specially designed for them; parents grouped together in one Christian society or another. A conscious effort was made not to associate with anyone who did not belong to the same class level and profess identical convictions.

In reality the walls of the ghetto, behind which "respectable families" sought refuge, proved to be very fragile. Parents and children had to encounter the "world" beyond the walls of the family or parish framework. The influence of the times was more harmful, especially on the young, because they were less prepared to confront it. Romantic literature abounds with dramatic stories of adultery and seduction in which the victims were the spoiled members of the best families. Those who preached against family traditions were pitilessly condemned. Under the pretext of not letting one stray sheep contaminate the whole flock, the elementary prescriptions of Christian charity were neglected.

Another harmful consequence of this ghetto attitude was the almost complete loss of any social influence. However pure their intentions might have been, Christian families must carry a considerable part of the responsibility for the grave crisis which family morality suffered during the two World Wars. More than political society, the family, under pain of infidelity to its vocation, must be an *open* society.

Children are members and not the property of the family. It seems in conformity with nature that the task of educating them, of making them men worthy of the name, falls in the first place to the family. The lamentable failure of the communist effort to transfer this mission to the state is a kind of a posteriori confirmation of what psychological analysis reveals. Education cannot stop with the development of the child's intellectual faculties. It must especially promote the development of moral and emotional faculties; this can only be done in a climate of love which, as we have seen, is the specific trait of the familial society. But the family has more duties than rights with respect to the child. Parents alone cannot decide upon what kind of education to give their children. The individual is not by nature only a member of his family; he is quite as much a member of the state and perhaps soon will also be a member of a veritable international society. It is thus inconceivable that parents could educate their children in a manner that runs counter to the fundamental principles of political unity. Thus, for example, parents could not morally raise their children to hate a given nation with which the state entertains friendly relations. Likewise, it is not morally admissible that a group of families found schools in which their children would be educated along the lines of hatred and class struggle.

The state, therefore, is quite within its rights when it demands a minimum of intellectual and civic education; and also when it exercises control over schools and programs of instruction, or even when it maintains its own schools. If families choose, for morally legitimate reasons, to send their children to a "private" school, that is to say one that does not come directly under the administration of the state, the latter does not for all of that lose its rights of control. The state on its part must respect the convictions of families so long as these are not contrary to the common good. This is particularly true of religious beliefs. Not that the state ought to promote any given religion; this would be quite contrary to the modern ideal of tolerance and the autonomy of the temporal. But neither the principle of tolerance nor that of separation of church and state postulates a contempt of the sacred.

It is a fact that harmony between the family and the state is difficult to realize. If political leaders are materialists or scientific rationalists they inevitably tend to impose their convictions upon the young. The problem is similar with respect to dissident groups in Catholic countries. In each concrete case much good will and adroitness is needed to reconcile the rights and interests of families with those of the state. And while these problems may be difficult they are not impossible to solve. Obviously there is no recipe that would be always and everywhere applicable. But the same is true in any domain of practical morality.

CHAPTER 20

On Truth and Falsehood

O NE OF the elementary moral demands is that our speech conform to our thought. Otherwise life in society would become impossible, for such life is in effect based on mutual trust. Now mutual trust could not exist if we were obliged to doubt or be forced to verify every affirmation and promise of others. There are, of course, mythomaniacs who often believe in their own lies; these may be said to lie in thought more than in word. It often happens that someone who is neurotically inclined will begin lying consciously to others, most frequently to impress them; but gradually he convinces himself and sincerely believes his own lies. One of my patients, the son of a small business man, affected an aristocratic background to succeed in Paris' world of high society. In the course of analysis he had difficulty remembering his parents and his real childhood. He could scarcely distinguish between his real and imaginative backgrounds. The fictive person he had become did not square with a man of modest background. What was objectively a lie had become a subjective truth for him. His words accorded with his thought but this latter did not accord with reality. And while the subjective truth of the schizophrenic has no connection with reality that of the neurotic is only partially unreal; he refuses to acknowledge only those aspects of reality that have emotionally disturbed him.

It is not good, as popular wisdom has it, to tell all the truth. However vital respect for the truth is for human society, it is not the supreme moral virtue. We have consistently stated that the true soul of genuine morality is charity, if some find this term too "religious," altruistic generosity. But there are some truths whose revelation would be radically contrary to charity. This is especially true since the motives for telling the truth are not always so much those of charity as of maliciousness, cowardice, and so forth. Anne, one of my patients, told her husband out of honesty that she was having an affair. But analysis revealed that she was very bitter toward her husband. She complained that he paid too little attention to her, gave her too small an allowance, and especially did not satisfy her sexually. She embarked upon an affair as much to satisfy her sexual urges as to wreak vengeance upon her husband. But vengeance isn't very effective if the deceived husband isn't aware of it. Whence the psychological impulse to confess, which her moral conscience had unconsciously disguised as love of the truth. Anne was furthermore very guilty about her affair. She hoped more or less confusedly that by telling her husband she would be punished and thus relieved of her guilt. Thus it turned out, in the complex of motivations that led Anne to reveal her adultery, that hatred of lying held a very insignificant place. But it was hard to convince her that it would have been more charitable had she not made her husband suffer by her confession and sought to relieve her guilt by some less sadistic, less impure means.

The moral obligation to tell the truth is, of course, not a merely utilitarian matter. Perhaps the following principles will be of some help:

1. Truth is a moral virtue in itself, independently of its utilitarian consequences. Only charity, the real love of others, can suspend the obligation in certain specific cases.

2. Normally we owe the truth to those who have the right to hear it. To conceal it from indiscreet persons cannot therefore be a lie in the moral sense of the word. Indeed often it is not enough to remain silent for this could be taken as tacit consent. A doctor, for example, who is asked by someone if a friend has syphilis, might legitimately say that he is treating the patient for

some other disease in order to spare him harmful suspiciousness. But the right, indeed the obligation of not revealing the truth is not limited to those who are professionally bound to secrecy. Particularly in those matters that concern others are we obliged to disclose the truth only to those, such as judges, who have a strict right to hear it.

3. In some cases we may conceal the truth from the individual it concerned if it will harm him. This principle enables us to give a possible answer to this frequently asked question: may one tell a patient the gravity of his disease? One can scarcely blame relatives for trying to spare a loved one the bitter truth. But this principle holds only in well-determined cases. I have known many cases where the patient, once he learned the seriousness of his condition, became very serene and made, in his last hours, remarkable spiritual progress. It matters little whether the doctor or the next of kin believe in the immortality of the soul. Their duty is to do nothing consciously that would count as an obstacle to what the patient may consider, at least subjectively, the summit of existential validity.

4. On the other hand, morality cannot approve the kind of lie that is frequently practiced by psychiatrists who propose, for example, to give their patients a "sleep cure" when in reality they intend to engage in more offensive therapeutic measures such as electro-shocks and narcosis. At the outside, such lying might be justified with serious psychotics who are incapable of comprehending their real situation. The neurotic can normally decide for himself what proposed therapeutic measures he will accept.

5. In court the witness ought to tell the truth even if this might harm one of his relatives. The common good justifies, and sometimes even demands, the sacrifice of the individual's good. But even this general rule suffers exceptions. It does, for example, in more or less revolutionary circumstances when society considers something criminal which is not morally a crime. This was the case with acts of resistance in France during the Nazi occupation. The courts appointed by the enemy had no right to the truth and

the witnesses were guilty of no moral wrong in remaining silent. We might add that the courts of all countries dispense those who are professionally bound to secrecy such as priests and doctors.

The numerous nuances that must be introduced in any consideration of the obligation to tell the truth make it the more difficult to carry out. There are two temptations in this respect: either to think that the obligation to tell the truth is determined only by personal motives or, secondly, to make the obligation so absolute that it suffers no exception. The first would lead to the total destruction of an elementary moral value that has great social utility. The second also implies serious dangers for both the individual and society. Here as in so many moral cases man must assume the total responsibility for his situation in the world; and we know that this is often ambiguous. But moral education ought to train men capable of making difficult decisions. To be sure, the risk of error will not be eliminated but this is also part of the human condition.

It is possible that a man not be able to recognize the truth or distinguish it from what is false. This is often the case with neurotics; only psychotherapy can help them. The same is true of the many victims of propaganda who lie only because they have been lied to. It is the moral duty of those who know the truth to enlighten them, to teach them to think correctly in order that they may speak truly.

The moral duty of telling the truth goes beyond the phenomenological level of consideration. All the moral virtues ought not only make us avoid evil but aid us in our pilgrimage toward existential truth. This should also be the case with respect to our duty to tend toward the discovery and recognition of the ultimate truth about our destiny and the destiny of the world. Metaphysical truth will also be a result of our moral duty.

CHAPTER 21

Blessed Are the Meek

THE CURRENT meaning of the words *"humility"* and *"pride"* is not of evangelical inspiration, although there is a widespread opinion to the contrary. From apostolic times preachers and Christian writers have praised humility and vituperated against pride. Christ himself was called "meek and humble of heart." But Christian moralists of ancient times understood by pride the *overestimation of self,* and by humility the *just estimation of self.* If we refer to modern preaching and pious literature we find that pride means the *just estimation of self* while humility signifies the *underestimation of self.* There is a great difference between the two conceptions.

Many men who love life and action revolt against what they take to be the Christian conception of humility; but it is not Christian; it is rather humility as conceived by Oriental sects and diffused in Western Christianity by the Cathars first of all and then by the Jansenists. Jansenism as a sect was very short-lived but, as is frequently the case, its influence has survived. It is only recently, in France at any rate, that we have gotten away from holding forth the example of a genius who out of humility declined the first place he would have merited by his talents; or some saint who out of humility affected simple-mindedness, and so on. It was understood, not so long ago, that anyone aspiring to spiritual perfection ought never seek the first places. Those who reached them washed their hands of responsibility by saying they were forced despite their efforts by their friends or by public opinion. Nietzsche is thus right in regretting that a man like Blaise Pascal did not realize his full potential because in the last period of his life he professed a kind of humility that prohibited ambition and success. But Nietzsche was wrong to blame Christianity for Pascal's failure. The blame must be laid squarely on Jansenism.

We have happily gone beyond that conception and today Christians do not hesitate to make full use of their talents whether in politics, art, or the intellectual life. Yet in certain very traditional quarters, particularly in religious communities for women, there is still a general confusion between humility and humiliation. Repugnant penances are imposed upon novices under the pretext of teaching them humility by humiliation. This is a serious illusion. The humiliated are in reality rarely humble. If the techniques of humiliation do not generate revolt, this is probably because the subject lacks vitality and normal aggression and will soon seek neurotic compensations. It is by no means a rare phenomenon that systematic humiliation ends with a puerile exaltation of pride or a sadomasochistic spirituality. There is the grubby pride of the publicans who ostentatiously dispute the last places; this pretence of humility is scarcely less ugly, nor more spiritually fruitful than the pride of the Pharisees whom Christ reproached for seeking the first places.

True humility, which ought to be promoted by the new morality, is according to the definition of a great medieval moralist, the recognition of the truth, the truth about one's self as well as about others. It demands that we recognize in all simplicity what we are and what we might become and thus act in consequence of this. The evangelical parable of the talents teach this kind of humility. God, or "nature"—gave each of us talents and potentialities unequal in quantity and quality. We have a strict mandate not to bury them, nor deny their existence, but to actualize them to the maximum. If we have occasion to render distinguished service to the human community, humility prohibits us from rejoicing in our talent; it rather demands that we recognize that we have only done our duty. Like all moral virtues, humility must be practiced not in the narrow perspective of individualism but in a communal perspective. True humility also directs us to be content if we fulfill a more modest role, provided we recognize that our talents are such. If we may compare the human race to a symphony orchestra it is quite normal that not everyone be a leader or play first violin. To do with as much perfection as possible the humblest of tasks contributes to the perfection of the whole.

The basis of true humility is thus self-knowledge. Since this is difficult it is much easier to allow oneself to be humiliated than to be truly humble. Humiliation can be affected by the techniques of pseudoeducation and these are easily learned and applied; but self-knowledge can only be learned through the psychological maturity of the subject himself.

A man who is aware of his worth and his talents is not proud unless he uses them egotistically for his own glorification and refuses to consider himself invested with a mission in the service of the human community. The proud man is egocentric. He considers himself the proprietor of his gifts and talents, a benefactor of mankind. He acts as though he were essentially superior to others, shows contempt for those less talented than he, and pretends to have the right to subjugate others, and indeed crush them with his superiority.

When the proud man's superiority is real we may admire him and indeed excuse his pride. But too often the egocentric possesses only an imaginary superiority. Those who are always promoting themselves and making themselves the center of attention are generally weak or neurotic and very unsure of themselves and thus become excessively concerned with what others think of them. In extreme cases the unconscious sentiment of worthlessness can lead the proud man to mythomania; he may pretend he is Napoleon or something of the sort. Such cases merit pity more than moral condemnation.

Vanity may be considered a puerile form of pride. Usually it is overcompensation for an inferiority complex. While the proud man seeks to impress others with what he has accomplished the vain man attaches too much importance to those insignificant and futile things that might distinguish him from the masses. He can easily become a liar.

It would be a mistake to confuse feminine coquetry with the vanity of the weak. We can certainly imagine a civilization in which woman's place will be radically changed, that is to say one in which she will no longer belong to the "second sex." In that eventuality coquetry would rightly receive harsh judgment at the hands of the moralists. But in the present state of things, in Western countries, some coquetry to emphasize woman's worth may be seen as not only morally permissible but morally necessary as well. We must, of course, regret the cult of stars which so frequently leads women to consider themselves primarily erotic objects and not human beings. In any event, we can scarcely call the absence of all coquetry in certain masculine type women as humility. For our part, we encourage those members of religious orders for women who affect some stylishness. There is no necessary connection between ugliness and the service of the Lord.

While morality condemns or at least disapproves of pride and its effects, it cannot but praise and encourage self-respect. It is absurd and inadmissible that a man be demanded in the name of humility not to be aware of his dignity as a man and not to take pride in his work. Self-respect in this sense ought never be confused with what simple folk call "pride" meaning thereby that so-and-so is vain, pretentious, and contemptuous.

CHAPTER 22

On Submission to Authority

EVEN IF we think St. Paul went a little far in recommending that Christians obey all governments, whether just or unjust, there can be no doubt that in principle obedience to legitimate authority constitutes a moral obligation. It is in effect the very condition of life in society. Perhaps one day men will reach such an elevated degree of spiritual maturity that, according to the dream of Kropotkin and other anarchists, the concepts of obedience and authority will no longer have any place since each individual will spontaneously seek the good of all. But for the present, and undoubtedly for a long time to come, we are far from that ideal.

Granted the principle of obedience there are still many problems in practice. Parents complain that their children no longer obey them; teachers have difficulty maintaining discipline in the classroom; military officers in increasing numbers refuse to obey the governments of their country, and that not only in Latin America! Finally, citizens in general tend more and more to ignore the duty of obedience.

The causes of this serious crisis are about the same as those of the moral crisis in general. With the secularization of social institutions and of individual consciences, authority has lost, by the force of things, its transcendent character. When St. Paul demanded that all Christians obey the pagan authority of Rome, he established the principle that all legitimate authority comes from God; thus the believer submits to God himself in obeying his parents, his teachers, or his government. We are not arguing that the secularization of institutions and consciences necessarily lead to the dissolution of authority. But perhaps this secularization took place too soon, before the human conscience evolved to a sufficient degree of maturity. Too, the consequences of individualism are far from having been overcome and in this perspective each makes himself the supreme judge of his actions.

On the other hand, the incontestable abuses committed by those who hold power are not unrelated to the fact that most men today consider obedience a purely negative obligation, a pure constraint. Under the pretext of holding their authority from God certain religious superiors and even popes demand an unconditional obedience from their subjects: *perinde ac cadaver*. Time-serving theologians have gone so far as to maintain the thesis that a religious ought to obey his superiors even when he is profoundly convinced that they are wrong; others extend the same principle to all faithful vis-à-vis ecclesiastical authority; whence is born anti-clericalism. Kings and emperors were obviously not to be outdone by popes and bishops in the matter of obedience. They abrogated divine investiture and demanded of their subjects an equally unconditional obedience. The same is true of military chiefs and fathers of families. That modern man, more aware of his individuality, has revolted against this kind of authoritarianism is easily enough understood. Some did so because they have ceased to believe in God, formerly thought to be the source of all authority. Others, by contrast, after having liberated themselves from all bonds of subordination to human authorities thought it quite logical to rise up against the supreme Authority. Believers still respect the principle of obedience—whether human or divine; but they refuse to obey blindly for they consider it contrary to their character as children of God.

Refusal to obey is not the only aspect of the moral question we are considering here. Excessive obedience can be just as harmful. Certain individuals as well as certain peoples are only too ready to consider as obedience what is in fact a lack of personal responsibility; this is how dictators are able to obtain such unconditional obedience from nations. Thus German soldiers and officers evinced genuine surprise when they were called to account for their crimes. Having accepted unconditional obedience to their Führer they believed (for the most part unconsciously) they could satisfy with impunity and in all good conscience their most perverse instincts. The example of the French in Algeria is an analogous case. An officer of the reserve, well-educated and leftist, admitted before a court that he did not understand how he could take such pleasure, even sadistic pleasure, in carrying out the tortures he was accused of. Under the cover of obedience he could give free reign to the primitive instincts of cruelty which his education had repressed but not destroyed nor genuinely sublimated. The only difference between the Germans and the French in this respect is that the latter were always morally reproached by their people while in Germany the collective conscience itself had made an act of submission to Hitler and to those who commanded in his name.

Since obedience is an indispensable moral virtue for the life of a society, moralists must inculcate it in the consciences of men. The serious abuses engendered by authoritarianism or blind obedience ought not deter them. The reform to be effected concerns those who hold authority perhaps more than those who must obey it. For as a matter of fact almost every man at one time or another finds himself now in a situation where he must obey and now in a situation where he must exercise authority.

Intelligent men ought never be asked to obey blindly, still more so unconditionally. Children may be required to make such submission but even here education ought as soon as possible point out the utility and the meaning of their obedience. For a much greater reason should this be so with adults. Constraint may be in order when we are dealing with antisocial types who deliberately refuse to conform to the laws and necessary conventions of society. But normal men ought to be asked to obey out of love for the good. Moreover, St. Paul himself distinguished between servile and filial obedience. Only the latter becomes a man aware of his dignity and his responsibilities; love of the good rather than love of authority should motivate our obedience.

I have often heard religious superiors complain about the lack of vocations. They generally blame it upon the lack of generosity on the part of young people today and an individualism which makes them refractory to the strict obedience religious life has traditionally demanded. Too, I know many women who, after a time in the convent, have renounced religious life because they found obedience too difficult.

As I understand the matter, the real difficulties with obedience have nothing to do with the lack of generosity on the part of young people today. The proof of this is that some congregations, like The Little Sisters of Jesus of Charles de Foucauld, have more postulants than they can accommodate; yet this order asks a generosity and self-sacrifice that exceeds what has been traditionally demanded. Likewise with many missionary orders, comprised primarily of young women of middle-class origin, who endeavor to bear evangelical witness in the poorest working sections of our large cities. All of these women, and many men too, are willing to obey religiously, but to obey *for something that is worth the trouble.* There aren't many today who show much admiration for the examples of obedience that abound in edifying hagiographies. If we read that an abbess sends a novice into a cold winter's night to look for her cat in the name of obedience we are more inclined to see an example of sadistic authoritarianism rather than a love of obedience. It is absurd to try to break the will of those striving for spiritual perfection by demanding the blind obedience of a slave. The will ought not be broken but put in the service of the good; and there is no good in slavery.

What we have said concerning the profound transformation that is taking place in the conception of religious obedience holds analogously for other forms of obedience and the exercise of authority.

CHAPTER 23

Sexual Morality

ALL WHO have attempted to study the problems of human sexuality with the same scientific objectivity and the same spirit of positive criticism that prevails in the study of any other problem of social or individual life have learned by bitter experience how easy it is to irritate public feeling and cause scandal. If psychoanalysis has for so long encountered much contempt and opposition it is not because of the less documented scientific theses of Sigmund Freud so much as because of his investigation of the sexual aspect of neurotic problems. Because Freud spoke of infantile sexuality, and put forth the hypothesis that the sexual instinct is operative in relations between parents and children, his system and his methods were a priori suspect. We are not in total agreement with Freud's theories of sexology and have subjected them to criticism in other works. But it is important here to insist on the fact that the violent opposition Freudian psychoanalysis encounters is not founded on previous scientific investigation but is of a strictly irrational and emotional origin.

Recently a French priest was interviewed on the problems of modern young people whom he was reputed to know very well. Speaking of certain practices of flirting very much in vogue he said that, all things considered, he would rather see them make love normally than engage in such degrading practices. When the journalist reported this opinion respectable people, and some not so respectable, were shocked. They neglected the context completely and focused on the thought that a priest dared say he would rather see young people make love!

This state of things is explained by the fact that sexual morality has evolved infinitely more slowly than other forms of morality. It remains almost completely rooted in ancestral taboos that have no rational justification whatsoever. Let us take the particularly significant example of onanism. Not only believers, who see in it a sin, but many unbelievers think they are doing something wrong in practicing it. Our intention is not to say that it is from all points of view praiseworthy. What interests us is *why* young people together with their educators and confessors consider it a moral fault. Most don't know why; others, particularly the clergy, say it is an unnatural act without being too clear what they mean by this statement. I shall thus try to clarify the problem by going back to the ancient myths whose "truths" continue to survive in our psychic unconscious. In ancient times many peoples, before they had any scientific knowledge of nature, attributed the active principle of procreation to the man alone; the woman was considered a mere passive receptacle. They believed that man's seed was a kind of participation in the divine creative power. It was therefore quite logical to consider all loss, particularly all voluntary loss of this precious seed a culpable waste of a divine gift. That is why Noah's grandson, Onan, was so severely reprimanded and bequeathed his name to one of the most agonizing taboos. Yet today no one attributes the same sacred character to the sperm. We know that of the millions of spermatazoids produced by each man, only a small percentage are destined for procreation while the others are wasted in one way or another with an astonishing prodigality. Already biologists are close to fecundating the ovule without any masculine intervention. If follows therefore that if morality is to take a stand on onanism, whether it be in the form of masturbation or interrupted intercourse, it must refer to principles that are more understandable to modern man than ancient taboos. Perhaps onanism is unnatural although that is by no means obvious; but if it is then it must be shown to be contrary to the *present* nature of man.

Some biologists and psychiatrists, very much aware of the harmful influence of sexual taboos on psychic health, have denounced sexual morality as such and proposed to reestablish human sexuality in its "biological simplicity." Animal sexuality, they argue, is not governed by morality and yet manifests far fewer deviations than human sexuality. Under the influence of civilization men have needlessly complicated the simple sexual instinct by linking it with a whole complex of feelings, including the divine and diabolic. Let us go back to "nature" and everything will work itself out! Some of the psychiatrists of a generation ago sincerely believed that the cure of neurosis necessarily implied the liberation of a sex instinct from all the controls and interdictions of morality; whence the aggravated conflict between modern depth psychology and those who remain convinced of the absolute character of morality and of sexual morality in particular.

In reality such psychiatrists and biologists are quite as mistaken on the nature of man as the conservative custodians of the moral order. Both conceive it as a static reality and consider the additions of evolution merely superfluous. Both believe that true human nature is to be found in the past with the difference that moralists would return to some supposed paradise from which man is said to have fallen while the psychiatrists and biologists would return to the animal past of our species. Both of these conceptions of human nature are equally retrograde and equally false.

There is no doubt that the sexual function is a biological one as normal and natural as any other biological function. There is nothing "divine" in it that would elevate us to the supernatural order nor nothing "demonic" that would enslave or annihilate us. The sexual instinct—and we grant this to the naturalists—is just as primitive as are the instincts of eating, drinking and breathing. But by virtue of its psychic development, of its accession to the *noosphere,* human nature has become more complicated and enriched not only in the sense that it added to its animal nature, which supposedly remains unchanged, various cultural superstructures but this animal nature itself has been fundamentally modified because of its intimate coexistence with the spirit. Only a false reductive method, which takes the most rudimentary for the most natural, would permit us to speak of human instincts as if they were essentially identical with animal instincts. All human instincts are intimately penetrated by the psyche. This is why purely psychic traumas can provoke respiratory and digestive troubles. And the more evolved man becomes, the more his biological instincts become biopsychic. If we try to deny this state of things we will end not with the "pure" animal nature but with a mutilation of human nature.

There is no doubt that man's sexuality has become more transformed by his psychic evolution than have his instincts of eating, drinking, or breathing. In man sex is inseparable from that supreme psychic function which we call *love*. Freudian psychoanalysis in trying to reduce love to a simple disguise of the sexual instinct, recognized in its own way the close overlapping of the two. But because of its false reductive method it cannot understand that the superior, far from being a simple disguise of the most primitive, can have its own reality which can transform the primitive to the point of making it unrecognizable.

It is not only dangerous but radically impossible to liberate morality from the psychic influence of human nature. We no longer consider relevant to morality such religious proscriptions as forbade a certain kind of food, whether absolutely, or on determined days. Yet morality has its word to say on abuses or excesses of food and drink as well as on the failure to nourish oneself sufficiently. Since sexuality has become the most psychic of the biological functions it follows in good logic that it, more than the others, pertains to morality.

Human sexuality, however different it be from animal sexuality, still retains the grandiose mission of transmitting life and thus assuring the continuation of the species. But as we noted in speaking of conjugal morality, human procreation must be closely controlled by "qualitative" as well as by "quantitative" morality. Unlike the animal state, human instinct is not a sure guide in either the choice of a partner nor in the frequency of fecundation.

But procreation is only one of the functions of human sexuality. The passion of love, which is at least theoretically inseparable from sexuality, has at all times inspired the most heroic actions as well as the most monstrous crimes. Without it most of our cultural masterpieces would never have seen the light of day and, consequently, the spiritual evolution of humanity would not be what it is. But without it, too, there would have been no Trojan war and King David would not have compromised his reputation with an abominable crime. It is not surprising that it has alternately been considered divine and demonic. The phallus has sometimes been adored as a god and sometimes construed as the most maleficent symbol. In any case, it is easy to see why peoples of all time have felt the obligation to submit sexuality, more than the other instincts, to strict moral control. Of course, the concrete prescriptions were not always the same. Sexual morality sometimes prohibited and sometimes permitted incest, polygamy, adultery in one or both spouses, homosexuality, and premarital relations. Moreover, some religions, including Catholicism, have demanded complete celibacy of their ministers. We do not intend to discuss the theoretical or practical motives of these different sexual moralities. It is sufficient for our purposes to note the universal consent on the necessity of such a morality. What is important is that we establish, in accordance with our means, the basis of a sexual morality which men of our times urgently need. This morality will evidently not be fundamentally different from sexual moralities of the past. It will be like them in the measure that man today is like man of the past. But in the measure that he is different he needs, if not new moral rules, at least new motives to follow the old rules.

To be *efficacious,* that is to say to effect that promotion of man to the order of the noosphere which we have taken to be the essential function of any morality worthy of the name, sexual morality cannot be purely negative. If it merely prohibits there is little chance that it will be respected by the educated man of

today. For modern man is too emancipated from religious traditions and beliefs to accept moral prescriptions simply because
they are the will of a God in whom he does not believe or the
conventions of a society which he can only accept after critical
verification. As for educated believers we have already noted that
they are largely liberated from a religion of fear; in their faith
as well as in the morality which it illuminates they seek strength
and positive reasons for living. The taboos may still exercise an
unconscious influence; but consciously the psychically mature
man desires the end of their domination.

We have had frequent occasion to say in these pages that the
foundation of all authentic morality is love, either natural generosity or supernatural charity. The moral value of a man ought
to be judged not in terms of his abstention from doing evil but
in terms of the degree of charity he manifests in his relations with
others. Since sexuality in psychically mature persons is of all their
faculties and all their instincts most indissolubly associated with
love it is in a privileged position to work for human promotion.
Perhaps the most serious error of Freudian psychoanalysis is to
consider the sexual instinct as tending toward the solitary pleasure of the individual while its orientation toward the other is
more or less by chance. In reality what most characterizes the sexual impulse is its tendency to establish a profound existential
bond with the other. In mature people, whose sexuality is most
impregnated with love, the bond thus created becomes more and
more spiritual; on rare occasions it reaches the sublimity that we
encounter in such saints as Francis of Assisi and St. Claire, Francis de Sales and Jeanne de Chantal, and others. In their case love
was totally exempt from carnal appetite but its sexual origin was
just as pronounced.

The adolescent, who must gather together all of his energies to
become fully himself, is generally turned in on himself and little
open to others. His sexual instincts take a narcissistic form: he
himself is the object of his libido. Masturbation, the sign par
excellence of autoeroticism, might be considered, at least statistically, as normal for the adolescent. Moralists of former times

were too ready to link it with moral turpitude, with sin. But this attitude can transform autoeroticism, in itself a simple biopsychic phenomenon, into a vice. Today we have happily become much more enlightened on this point for few priests or educators are as set against the "solitary vice" as they at one time were. We are quite sure that this development will have happy effects on the moral plane.

Normally, at about fifteen or sixteen years of age, the sex impulse begins to direct itself toward others, toward a person of the opposite sex, and to become integrated with love. By virtue of this the young man and the young woman gradually emerge from their narcissistic "shell," become open by the intermediary of the object of their love to people in general, to the world and to the concrete life as it is lived about them (while as adolescents they lived in a largely imaginary world), and become capable of disinterest and true generosity. The love of one person is like an apprenticeship to universal love. St. John already warned us about pretending to love the whole universe without loving our neighbor. Such love of humanity is abstract, without warmth, and frequently goes hand in hand with real cruelty toward others as we observe in the life of a Robespierre and other seekers after an ideal "purity."

Autoeroticism, whether or not it manifests itself in masturbation, begins to be a moral problem when it goes beyond adolescence. It then stops up the release of emotional energies, inhibits the natural generosity of man, and renders the subject inept for love of an individual person, for humanity, and the common good. Every time I meet a markedly egocentric person I suspect him of being autoerotic; in those cases I have been able to verify I have never yet been wrong.

Thus the "new morality" also considers autoeroticism an evil, but not because it turns the seed, supposedly so precious, away from its "normal end" but because it prevents the blossoming of that generosity and love without which man cannot be authentically moral. Moreover, the narcissistic fixation is often the cause of serious psychic troubles. To make our position clear on this important problem, let us note that frequently autoeroticism is perfectly "chaste," that is to say unaccompanied by masturbation; this is especially true of women. Current morality considers such chastity a virtue; but quite different is our point of view.

The most frequent cause of the narcissistic fixation is an unconscious guilt feeling which generally follows upon the mistakes made by parents and clergy in handling the adolescent's problem of masturbation. But there are other causes as well; for example, the parents refusal to let their child indulge its natural curiosity about the world under the pretext that his "virtue" would be endangered. A mother who is too attached to her child and endeavors to give him everything herself without help from the outside also creates the conditions under which the child will find it very difficult to become really great.

In our experience it seems that homosexuality is also most frequently the result of an autoerotic fixation. A person of the same sex is not really an *other*. If a young person feels attracted to a person of the same sex it is because something deep in his psyche inhibits the natural élan toward a true *other*, toward a person of the other sex. It follows that homosexuals, although less than those who love no one at all, that is to say, totally narcissistic persons, are excessively introverted, and are insufficiently interested in the outside world. Only artistic creation seems to be uninhibited by homosexuality; and this, of course, can be a means of attaining moral superiority. But the gift of artistic creation is not given to everyone, nor is it specifically the gift of the introverted.

As long as we see in sex primarily a source of dangers and temptations, which morality would supposedly reduce, there can be no question of an authentic sexual morality. What we have already said should convince the reader that human sex must be considered as an existential value. Morality certainly disapproves with good reason the diversion of sexual energy from its role as a creator of values; but it must also disapprove the mutilation, whether psychic or physical, of a *moral function* that is just as important.

In many religions monastic life requires complete chastity. This is true of the great religions of the Orient; it was true of the Essenes and other hermits and cenobites of Judaism; it is likewise true of Christianity. In the latter religion the obligation of celibacy has gradually extended, under the influence of the monks, to the whole clergy. Since the clergy has always been charged with the intellectual and moral formation of the faithful their influence could not but be decisive.

We don't propose to discuss the reasons why the Catholic Church makes this demand of her clergy. Practically speaking, everyone is free to enter the religious life and can, with full knowledge of the causes, accept or not the obligations of this state. But it is important to understand that it is psychologically normal that clerics see the moral and spiritual excellence of chastity in proportion to the difficulty of its practice. Whence the tendency to overemphasize chastity and consider those who don't practice it morally inferior. Let us point out, however, that the Catholic Church has never adopted the doctrine of those numerous "pure" sects that are always springing up within Christianity which completely anathematize sexuality. Yet many preachers and authors of pious books still exalt virginity, chastity, and celibacy to a degree that makes those who don't practice them feel inferior and guilty, like second-class Christians. There have been married saints but writers of spiritual biographies are careful to point out that they sanctified themselves because they followed the example of the monks. Thus we praise Anna Maria Taigi, a saintly mother of Napoleonic times, for having sexual intercourse with her brutal husband only because he demanded it. Only recently has official Catholicism taken positive steps to understand and make understood the dynamic moral force of sexuality which is immoral only in the bad use we make of it.

As a physiological fact virginity has no moral significance whatever. The Church honors numerous saints as "virgins and martyrs" who were not virgins in the physical sense of the term. Many of the early saints, who were violated by their executioners, are honored as virgins. Nor would any Christian refuse the title of virgin, in the moral and religious sense, to those Belgian religious who were recently violated by Congolese soldiers. In the same moral and religious sense, it would be impossible to consider virgins those modern young women who engage in all sorts of erotic pleasures, although taking great care to safeguard their physical virginity, for the sole motive of trapping a husband. That men value this kind of virginity in no way indicates moral superiority; it simply reveals that they are still victims of ancient taboos.

Chastity represents a high moral value if we understand it as a certain discipline and moderation in sexual activity; that is to say, as the opposite of lust. Nor does sexual abstinence imply a loss of the capacity to love; quite the contrary, the energies thus liberated can be sublimated in the true sense of the word and directed to superior forms of love. If chastity meant merely the interdiction of all sexual activity, it would be moral only to the degree that the motives for abstention were moral. The religious who remains chaste in order to put all of his emotional faculties in the service of spiritual perfection and altruistic dedication to others may rightly be considered to practice a superior morality. Likewise a woman, whose husband is a prisoner of war, who remains chaste out of love for him is acting morally. In both cases what is moral is not the absence of sex, in itself perfectly legitimate, but the aspiration, in the first case, to spiritual perfection and, in the second, fidelity to a loved one. On the other hand, there are men and women who are chaste for lack of opportunity to be otherwise; their chastity is neither morally good nor bad. Others are chaste for reasons of egoism, because they refuse to or are incapable of love; their chastity is immoral. Voluntary chastity which is justified by no higher generosity is often the equivalent of a perversion; morality cannot approve it any more than it could approve some other form of psychic or physical perversion.

Sexual relations which are not inspired by the mutual love of the partners can never be moral. *Rational* unions, that is to say marriages founded on material or moral interests but not on love were morally tolerable as long as men and women had not attained a very high degree of emotional maturity, of personal awareness. For the same reason this tolerance extends to simple men and women today. But it is intolerable among emotionally adult persons. Each time they "make love" without loving, they sin against their human dignity, against the holy law of spiritual evolution.

It is paradoxical, in this perspective, that so many moralists and other zealous partisans of the moral order condemn so severely solitary onanism and sexual relations between those who love one another but are not married while they are extremely tolerant of prostitution. In Europe legal prostitution lasted longest in those countries in which the Church exercised a determining influence on legislation. And generally speaking the initative to close houses of prostitution was not taken by Catholic officials. In France no self-respecting politician would dare vote for the abolition of the law of 1920 which forbade the publicizing or selling of contraceptives; but these same self-respecting, but terribly hypocritical, politicians campaign—clandestinely, of course—from time to time in favor of reopening the houses of prostitution. One wonders whether or not in some quarters the fear of love is not greater than the fear of sexual sins.

Whatever be our judgment on "free love" we must admit that prostitution is incomparably more immoral. For here no emotional bond exists between the partners; the woman is robbed of her dignity as a person, reduced to the status of mere merchandise, a simple instrument of selfish pleasure for man, without any possibility of spiritual participation. It is rather bewildering that those who condemned slavery and the condition of the proletariat in the name of morality tolerated prostitution until the middle of the twentieth century and continue to look upon it more or less benevolently. Morality can find extenuating circumstances for the prostitute but none for those who make use of her "services" or a society which tolerates prostitution.

CHAPTER 24

Conjugal Morality

CONJUGAL MORALITY is not merely a subchapter of sexual morality. It is true that marriage is the normal framework within which love, both carnal and spiritual, develops between man and woman and only in rare exceptions is there justification for "platonic marriages" founded on spiritual love alone and excluding carnal relations. But marriage is in fact and by right much more than the socially and morally normal state for the development of love. It has the responsibility of founding and making prosper the family, what we have called the "fundamental moral unity." Some rather muddled theoreticians have advocated the abolition of marriage in the name of "the sacred rights of the individual," as they have condemned the vows of religion and any other commitment that binds man in a stable manner. But today we are much less convinced than were those who lived in the nineteenth century of the merits of individualism. Quite the contrary, our firm conviction is that the isolated individual who is free of all commitment is a mere abstraction and that every effort to make him an existential reality is doomed to failure. Consequently there are not many today who question the value of marriage as an institution, at least in principle. It guarantees the stability and the solidity of family structures; children and parents can find there, or at least ought to find, that climate of affection and security that is necessary to their normal growth.

But we must admit that the walls of this venerable edifice are weakening. It has become mandatory to rethink the morality of marriage. In this short chapter we can do no more than focus attention on those aspects of the problem that appear to us most controversial or upon which we have especially reflected. In the past few years there have been many excellent books on the moral problems of marriage. I should like to recommend in particular *Morality and Conjugal Life* by A. M. Henry O.P. Although the author writes as a theologian and thus adopts a point of view quite different from that of a psychologist, we are in almost total agreement with his insights and conclusions.

Like all decisive human commitments, marriage must be looked upon as a vocation, that is to say as the best way for a given person to realize his human potentialities, both on the natural and transcendent planes. Again we are evidently speaking of those who have transcended the stage of preexistential banality and who are conscious of their belonging to the noosphere. For those who are not so evolved marriage is primarily a biosociological function, a function which the more evolved person does not deny but integrates in a higher communal and personal synthesis. It follows that for psychically adult persons there is no morality except a marriage of love.

We have noted that sexual union can only be morally justified by love. And while marriage is the natural place for sexual union it is charged, as we have said, with several other highly human functions. Only a marriage of love has the necessary dynamism to overcome individual egoisms, to inspire that self-sacrifice which is indispensable if men and women who are demanding with respect to themselves and life are not to be deceived.

By love we evidently do not mean that superficial flame of the senses which we popularly refer to as a "bolt from the blue." One of the principal reasons for the present crisis of conjugal morality is precisely the too frequent confusion between a bolt from the blue and love. Because two young people who are psychically immature experience a violent physical attraction for one another they think they are in love and get married. But the sensual flame generally lasts about as long as a straw fire. The young married couple soon realize that they have nothing to say to one another, that no deep harmony exists between them, that the physical attraction itself has vanished. Then it is divorce with its drama and its misery or, if they do not divorce one another, they have nothing to look forward to but a monotonous and boring life side by side—a state that is at best amoral.

True love, of course, implies physical attraction but the communication of minds is equally important. Only this can constitute the stable foundation of a conjugal union. It is capable of intensifying and prolonging sensual harmony but it is very rare that sensual harmony can give birth to spiritual harmony. And when, at length, age and habit diminishes sensual attraction in a marriage founded on true love, the harmony of temperaments will continue to furnish the couple with the energies necessary to the fulfillment of their vocation, a vocation which can be as sublime as any religious vocation and is certainly just as difficult.

Need we insist on the truth that the married vocation demands as much psychic and emotional maturity as a religious vocation? Marriage between those who are emotional adolescents can succeed, at least on the objective and sociological level, only if it is part of a strongly structured social and family context, drawing strength from solid traditions and convictions. But such milieus are becoming more and more rare; in normal situations the couple have only themselves to count on and this is often not enough. But it would not do to legislate in the name of morality a minimum age for marriage for not everyone matures at the same pace. Generally speaking, workers and peasants, who are early confronted with the realities and responsibilities of life, are as mature at twenty as most of the bourgeois and intellectuals are at thirty.

Once given the essential condition of love it is also well to take into account certain objective factors before marrying: finances, family and social background, health, education, and so forth. Today an approximate equality of education seems particularly important for more than the other factors ennumerated it is the condition of authentic communication between two people.

The stability of the marital bond is postulated by the very nature of marriage. None of the moral benefits marriage must promote could be attained if this were not the case. In principle then conjugal morality cannot recommend divorce as a normal solution to the difficulties encountered in marriage. The only question that might be asked is whether this principle must be adhered to with the intransigence of the Catholic Church or whether after all there might not be certain justifiable exceptions.

We noted earlier that morality, even the demanding Christian morality, admits of exceptions to the divine precept: *Thou shalt not kill;* yet the sacred character of life is not therefore compromised. In our opinion there can be, and effectively are, cases where divorce, the separation of husband and wife, seems mandatory in the name of conjugal morality itself. If the continuation of the marital union only interfered with the development of one or another of the parents, we could still argue that such is the risk they assumed in marrying, that they ought to have known each other better before taking the decision, that marriage is too important a social institution to sacrifice to the happiness of individuals. But it is not only a question of the happiness and development of the parents; there are the children to be considered. And often separation is necessary for their sakes. Indeed, even the Catholic Church tolerates separation in serious cases, even when it is legalized as divorce. But she will not permit the parties involved to remarry.

We cannot contest the Church's right to demand even heroic virtue of her members. What is paradoxical is that the Church is much less rigorous in applying other moral principles whose sacred character is not less evident. An example would be the case already mentioned of killing. We know, too, that in the past high-placed ecclesiastics have often been quite accommodating when it is a question of "annulling" the marriage of some king or powerful lord. However that may be, every priest knows of the painful dramas that result from this intransigence, even among fervent believers, without mentioning the hypocrisy which it frequently encourages. I am thinking of a good Catholic whose wife abandoned him and their four small children. Despite his good will he was forced to admit after a time that chastity was impossible for him; this difficulty was complicated by his loneliness and the problems of raising his children. Should he follow the path of so many others and seek sexual satisfaction in more or less ephemeral affairs? No priest would refuse him absolution for such indulgences and he could continue being the respectable Catholic he had always been. Our friend could not abide such hypocrisy. He remarried and was by that fact excluded from the communion of the faithful. This is one case among thousands; we would like to see the Catholic hierarchy consider this problem with all the Christian charity at their disposal.

A much more controversial question in the eyes of the majority of our contemporaries is the Catholic Church's fierce opposition to the divorce of those who are not really believers. When we consider that in Catholic countries many marry in the Church not to receive the sacrament, which means nothing to them, but uniquely for reasons of convenience isn't it pure fiction to consider them married religiously? To say that they are married "by natural law" and that this law also requires the stability of the marital bond is, of course, true. But, again, this same law forbids killing with equal rigor. There is no doubt that legal tolerance of divorce can lead to abuses that could be a serious threat to the fundamental social cell that is the family; far be it from us to advocate marriages à la Hollywood that last about as long as the whim that motivated them. Our only point is this: a *personalist* and *communal* morality cannot be constrained by the rigid principle of all or nothing.

When the human conscience was more social than personal, moralists considered procreation the primary if not the only end of marriage; they tended further to see in this the only justification of sexual intercourse. St. Paul and those moralists who follow him might appear very large-minded because they also tolerate marriage as a solution to the "concupiscence of the flesh."

For some fifty years now many moralists have been aware of the evolution of conscience toward greater personalization. Dr. Doms, a German theologian, was one of the first to argue that marriage has two primary ends of equal moral value. The *subjective* end would be to promote the mutual love of the parents and the *objective,* social end, would be procreation. In France the Christian family movement under the direction of Father Violet adopted the same perspective and I don't think I am mistaken in attributing the happiness of many Christian homes to its influence. No impartial observer can fail to note that the union of hearts is much more generalized in families today than in preceding generations; this is because of the moral and spiritual reevaluation of conjugal love. The expression "marital duty" was well-known to our parents; but it is scarcely mentioned today without a touch of irony.

The fact that most people marry today because they love one another rather than to have children does not mean that children are excluded. Quite the contrary; in many countries marriages of love have more children than the earlier bourgeois marriages of reason which frequently limited themselves to one child. Couples united in love see in children the normal realization of that love.

Couples today do not want their families to be a result of biological determinism. Morality, one of whose most noble functions is to promote man along the way of the spirit and therefore of liberty, obviously cannot disapprove of this tendency. Paternity and maternity are truly human only when they are founded upon the free consent of the interested parties. Of course this liberty can be affirmed, and often is, in an a posteriori manner as a ratification of what was not previously willed but was consequently accepted generously. But it is still more in accordance with the spiritual nature of man that the children be positively wanted, that parents be able to decide how many children they are going to have and, insofar as possible, be able to space them accordingly.

That the limiting and control of births appeared immoral, and was condemned as such, in biblical times is perfectly understandable. There was no population explosion then and children were the principal source of family income. Moreover, the infant mortality rate was high and in this way nature effected a kind of control of her own. In the days of our grandparents it was common for more than a dozen children to be born into a family of whom only three or four reached adulthood. The problem is quite different today. The three billion inhabitants of the earth, soon to become six billion, although unequally distributed from country to country, overpopulate our planet. Modern medicine has greatly decreased the infant mortality rate and has prolonged life expectancy. Let us hope too that our accession to the noosphere will soon eliminate that other factor of "natural" selection which is war. It is true, science is capable of appreciably increasing the quality and quantity of our means of subsistence. But it does not seem that this progress can keep pace with the population increase. The most able and conscientious sociologists and economists are alarmed and we must take them seriously. As long as we have not found the means to check significantly the birth rate in Asia, in certain countries of Latin America, and in Africa, all our efforts for social progress, welfare, and peace will be doomed to failure.

The same problem exists, although in a different form, in developed countries. For the time being the United States and the countries of Western Europe have enough resources to enable their citizens to live comfortably; these countries could accommodate an increase in their populations. But if the birth rate is not controlled, in the present state of hygiene, the population of these countries will soon double and even triple. But economics is only one aspect of the problem. The material progress of these countries is accompanied by progress of the personal conscience. Aware of having triumphed to some degree over physical determinism, men and women no longer want to submit to biological determinism. They want to have children but they want to raise them comfortably and reserve the right to determine how many they will have.

One cannot but laud an aspiration that is so manifestly in line with the evolution of humanity. The debate is not therefore one of principle but concerns the means of application.

Let us hope that everyone agrees that it is immoral to refuse to have children out of pure egoism, and this independently of the means used to carry out such a resolve. Supposing there is no lack of generosity, the most moral and most natural means of birth control is periodic continence; it is also the only absolutely sure means. But this method is qualified by several moral restrictions. For example, it must be a mutual decision. Even granted this, prolonged continence can cause dangerous physical or psychic disturbances for one or both of the parties and thus endanger the harmony of their marriage.

It is not true that all Catholic moralists are "natalists." Most of them are sufficiently aware of the problem to be favorable to free paternity and maternity. They are however of the opinion that the sexual act must be "according to the laws of nature." Consequently, continence is the only means of limiting and spacing births. They have no right to recommend total or even prolonged chastity to couples. But the woman is fecund for only a few days during the menstrual cycle and due to the work of Ogino and others we are in a position to determine this period with quasi-certitude. Thus most confessors recommend abstinence from sexual relations during this short period. Unfortunately the "rhythm method" promises more than it can deliver. Too many women have irregular cycles to apply this method with any degree of certainty. It further implies calculations that are hard to reconcile with the spontaneity of love. The day therefore must come, and we hope as soon as possible, when Catholic moralists will recognize that continence is not the only morally licit means of solving the pressing problem of birth control. The moralist has no business trying to invent improvements upon the rhythm method; this is the work of doctors, biologists, and sociologists. It is enough that moralists shake off the influence of taboos and come to a more accurate understanding of human nature and of human sexuality in particular. In this way they will be less of a stumbling block to the work of specialists. It is essential to recall here that in this case, as in others, the criterion of morality is not in material facts and techniques but in generosity of hearts. We only wish to add that, from a moral as well as a medical and psychological point of view, there is no common denominator between contraception and abortion. Religious moralists are simply wrong to insist upon such a parallel. By doing so they actually defeat their own purpose for many conclude that, since contraception is a general and normal practice, abortion can't be any worse. But there is a great difference. In the first case it is a question of not giving life, a position that is easily justified when we admit that procreation is not the sole function of human sexuality. In the second case, it is a question of destroying life.

CHAPTER 25

The Moral Value of Asceticism

IT MIGHT be wondered whether the "new morality," as we have defined it in this book, isn't too positive, giving too much importance to success, the joy of living and creating, personal and communal fulfillment. We are quite certain that we will be accused of precisely this. And apparently rightly so since all past and present moralities have insisted on the necessity of mortification and sacrifice, of renouncement and penance. Only at this price, it is argued, can moral perfection lead to the supreme perfection which is sanctity.

We are neither ignorant of nor denigrate the moral value of asceticism, of penance, and renouncement. But it does not seem to us that these should be emphasized in a morality of man that promotes existential reality. A good number of people today have turned their backs upon traditional religious morality because they feel it is too negative, that it is of little help to them in their problems. As a matter of fact, because of the many abuses of which asceticism has been guilty in the past, it is important to insist that neither sacrifices nor renouncement are moral *in themselves;* they are mere means, and their moral value depends on the end they serve. Thus penance has high moral value when it leads to true *metanoia,* that is to say a renewed orientation of our lives. But any well-informed confessor knows that all too frequently it is merely a pretext for more or less conscious masochistic tendencies. Sacrifice also is morally excellent in the case, for example, of a scholar who sacrifices his health and his life in order that mankind may benefit by his discoveries. The mother who keeps vigil over her sick child's bed is certainly acting very morally. But we know that we can sacrifice ourselves for causes that have no moral value at all, which are indeed clearly immoral. Thus national socialism in Germany had its heroes who sacrificed their leisure, their health, and their lives for the cause they served. But since the cause was bad there seems no way we can attribute moral value to their sacrifices. It seems in order to insist upon these obvious points, for morality has become far too subjective, to the point of completely neglecting the objective meaning of behavior.

In itself, to renounce something that appears good, useful, or simply agreeable to us is in no way moral. Frequently, this kind of detachment is more or less openly neurotic and when it implies, as it frequently does, a contempt of what is good and beautiful then it is immoral. It quite often happens that pride and avarice lurk behind the virtuous façade of detachment and renouncement.

Teilhard de Chardin is perfectly right when he says that as long as we possess nothing we have nothing we can renounce or sacrifice. From what could we be detached when we are attached to nothing? It is important therefore to actualize all our potentialities, to love ardently all that is good and beautiful, without rejecting what is simply pleasant. It is only *afterward,* in a kind of second movement of the dialectic of moral progress, that renouncement, detachment, sacrifice, and asceticism can take on any concrete meaning, can become genuine moral values.

We are not arguing that methodical asceticism, with appropriate techniques, is never necessary; it quite possibly is for those who are striving for spiritual perfection. On the moral plane, however, it is above all the renouncements and detachments which daily life imposes which must be given value. We love the world and want to enjoy what is good and beautiful in it. But irreconcilable things may attract us without either of them being bad. Thus, for example, one cannot simultaneously enjoy life in the city and in the country or be married and totally independent, and so forth. Life imposes choices and every choice by the nature of things implies renouncement.

Supposing we have done everything in our power to accomplish our task in the great work of universal creation; we have tried to combat evil in all of its forms and promote the good. Yet it might be that the result corresponds neither to our desires nor to our efforts and hopes; perhaps all our efforts have failed. Or, again, what we believed was a summit was only a hill and our strength does not permit us to climb them all. The temptation in the face of such failures and inadequacies would be to resign ourselves, to succumb to discouragement. We perhaps thought we were geniuses, called to realize masterpieces, and yet experience has made it clear that we are but modestly gifted. To be able to renounce illusions, to never grow discouraged before difficulties, to do our work as men however humble it be—this seems to be the most authentic moral asceticism. There is nothing unhealthy about it; nor is there any conflict between creative work and joy in living. Such asceticism does not prohibit us from becoming attached to creatures and things for it is in proportion to our attachment that our indispensable detachment will be more or less great; it enables us to go out of ourselves to become part of the universal whole.

Morality disapproves egocentric attachment to what we are or what we do. Let us recall the evangelical parable about the husbandman who accumulated great riches and hoarded grain in his barns against the day of insecurity. It did not occur to him that he might die just when he was ready to begin the good life. Whatever we have realized, in ourselves or in the world, we must know how to be detached in order to go on ahead to new tasks. I remember an old friend who began the study of Greek at the age of eighty-five; he had led a full life but he was convinced that he did not deserve to rest, that there were many things yet to do.

The most precious human good is obviously our life itself. We ought to love it and live it fully. But we early become aware that life in this world will not last eternally and that one day we will have to become detached from it too. Yet this is not a motive for discouragement, sadness, or inaction. Usually it is the man who loves life most passionately and realizes great things in it who confronts death most joyously, while he who is greedy with his money, his time, and his energies is imprisoned by his miserable life, fears the very thought of death, revolts against a God (or fate) who does not permit him to vegetate indefinitely in this world which he has never loved properly anyway nor really enjoyed its goods or its beauties.

CHAPTER 26

Moral Education

I N THE first part of this work we said that man is a moral being as much as he is a being endowed with reason and speech. But we ought not conclude with Jean Jacques Rousseau that, to assure the perfect moral development of the individual, we should let the moral instinct act in a perfectly free manner. In this perspective all immorality is blamed upon the constraints and malfunctions which society imposes upon human nature. Rousseau's conception of nature and morality is wrong because he fails to see that since man evolved out of the animal state, that is to say since he became man, there is no such thing as a "pure instinct." If our instincts were left to themselves, without any control on the part of the spirit, they would surely attain their natural object; but their chances of deviation and perversion would be proportionately great. An animal does not eat or drink more than is necessary but man is capable of committing such excesses if he does not control himself by his reason and will. Still less, as we noted, can man trust his sexual instinct. The moral instinct, the most humanized of all, does not function with more sureness. Man must therefore learn to master and utilize his instincts. He must be educated to know how much to eat, how to organize his sexual energies, and so forth.

Moral education must begin very early, practically in infancy. We would be seriously mistaken to think that religious education consists only in the teaching of theology. We must be careful, too, not to confuse moral education with the teaching of an ethical theory; there is no need to inculcate the child with "principles." Moral education ought first of all to act upon the automatic reflexes of the child and help him form *moral habits*. Then, in the measure of his emotional and intellectual maturity, he must be taught to love the good.

The most efficacious "method" or "technique" of moral education is parental example; so much the better if this is reinforced and confirmed by society. Without this example there is good reason to fear that all other methods will fail. How could selfish parents inspire altruism in their children? How could unfaithful parents encourage fidelity in their children? A business man I know, who became something of a specialist on the black market during the war, could not understand how his only son ("who lacked nothing and was educated by religious") could have become a "leather jacket" and finally be condemned by the courts for various crimes. But given the family background of this young man it would be surprising if he had turned out any other way. Educators and other outside influences can counteract bad family example but only in exceptional cases.

An adage has it that each country gets the government it deserves. With equal justice it might be said that each country or each age gets the young people it deserves. Is it surprising that soldiers who have been taught to kill and torture continue to act immorally after they have been demobilized?

Moral education ought not be separated from the formation of the person as a whole. All compartmentalization of the personality is harmful. Moral education goes hand in hand with intellectual education but especially with emotional education. We do not share the current prejudice, which is a reaction to earlier prejudices, which condemns outrightly punishment and reward in moral education. Prudently used such methods can efficaciously contribute to the formation of "good habits" in the child, particularly in the early stages. But rewards and punishments are merely accessory tools; if too much emphasis is placed on them we risk developing a purely conformist and utilitarian personality which may prevent the individual from doing harm to others but will scarcely help him achieve a superior moral life.

By the example which they give, an example that can be explicated and confirmed by words, educators should strive to impart the conviction that the good is more attractive than evil, that it gives as much joy and ought therefore be loved. Great efforts, sometimes physical but more often psychic, are necessary to overcome our egoism and penchant for evil. But it is not difficult to convince children or adolescents that such effort, far from being a mutilation of nature, is a fulfillment because it is on the side of Life. It is important to convey the love of life for only those who love life, and find it beautiful are capable of authentic morality. I know families in which the most rigorous respect for moral proscriptions reigns. Unfortunately too much emphasis is put on their austerity thus giving the impression that it is difficult and painful to follow the good. There is so much insistence on the temptations of evil that unconsciously the children feel more and more attracted to it and end by regarding moral duty as burdensome, as an obstacle to life. This psychological process explains the moral failures of so many who come from "good homes." The end of moral education is not to prevent young people from making mistakes but to give them the desire to do what is beautiful, great, and good.

Educators ought not forget that their duty is to form future adults, persons capable of acting morally by themselves, and confronting their duties as men and as members of the human community. Children must therefore be educated progressively, in the measure of their general maturity, to the increasing responsibility of their actions until they are able to assume full responsibility for their lives, for their condition as *beings in the world*. To this end it is necessary that the child become aware as soon as possible of his solidarity with others, that he is responsible for others, that there is more joy in giving than in receiving. This indispensable formation in generosity is evidently easier in larger families than in those of one child. An only child will quite naturally consider himself the center of the universe and believe that everything is due to him while he owes nobody anything. In this case the school and different clubs can supply for the deficiences of family education just as they can also second the efforts of larger families which tend to become closed societies.

It is extremely important for the success of moral education that a spirit of loyalty and trust prevail in the family, in the school, and in youth movements. Dissimulation, which is so contrary to youth's natural frankness, almost always causes considerable harm. Children and adolescents must be trusted even when we know there will be occasional abuses. I have known serious problems to develop because parents and educators opened letters received by adolescents. Other problems are precipitated by educators' refusal to believe a child's protest of innocence with respect to some misdemeanor. As long as there is no definitive proof of the child's guilt it is much preferable to believe him, even though we are wrong, than to run the risk of losing his confidence.

What should be the place of religion in moral education? Undoubtedly as a reaction against former abuses, many Christian parents today tend to make too radical a separation between morality and religion. They are a little like those Christian scholars who pretend to divorce their faith totally from their scholarly work. These parents try to make their children love the good because it is the good and avoid as much as possible reference to God. It seems to us there is a misunderstanding here.

To be sure, God must not be reduced to the role of a mere custodian of morality. Children must not be given the impression that He is a kind of superprotector of the peace or a superwatchman of public gardens. At all costs we should avoid telling children who lie or disobey that they "hurt the baby Jesus." Above all, they must not be threatened with the fires of hell for committing "impure acts." Neither religion nor morality will gain anything from this kind of confusion and both stand to lose a good deal. Moreover, parents and educators whose own faith is not very lively have no right to appeal to God-as-guardian-of-the-moral-order. The idea so dear to Voltaire that *"religion is necessary for the people"* is both false and morally dangerous. That is why we think it wrong, just as harmful to religion as to morality, to oblige nonbelieving teachers to teach religion in the school.

On the other hand, it seems very desirable that religion be enlisted in the service of moral education in those families, schools, and movements that are authentically Christian. Not of course to corroborate a system of rewards and punishments but as a means of offering young people a more elevated ideal, a more sublime conception of human destiny and universal fraternity.